# THE ARDENT PILGRIM

# THE ARDENT PILGRIM

*An Introduction to the Life and Work of
Mohammed Iqbal*

IQBAL SINGH

DELHI
OXFORD UNIVERSITY PRESS
CALCUTTA CHENNAI MUMBAI
1997

Oxford University Press, Walton Street, Oxford OX2 6DP
Oxford New York
Athens Auckland Bangkok Calcutta
Cape Town Chennai Dar es Salaam Delhi
Florence Hong Kong Istanbul Karachi
Kuala Lumpur Madrid Melbourne Mexico City
Mumbai Nairobi Paris Singapore
Taipei Tokyo Toronto
and associates in
Berlin Ibadan

First Published by Longmans, Green and Co. Ltd., London 1951
This edition © Oxford University Press 1997

ISBN 0 19 563979 0

Typeset by Sakshi DTP Option, Rohini, Delhi 110085
Printed in India at Pauls Press, New Delhi 110020
and published by Manzar Khan, Oxford University Press
YMCA Library Building, Jai Singh Road, New Delhi 110001

*To the memory of*
*Malang (Dr Nazir Ahmed Shah)*
*and*
*Rashid Anwar*

# Preface to the First Edition

It is customary in India to invest public figures with legendary haloes even during their lifetime. No posthumous probation is required of them to qualify for their proper niches in the national pantheon. Biography, therefore, still remains largely a branch of hagiography; portraiture is expected for the most part to conform strictly with the stylized conventions of an hieratic tradition. The result is that we are presented with waxwork models of impeccable virtue which are no doubt immensely edifying and exalting for all those who seek edification and exaltation, but in which it is hard to recognize the light and shade, the subtle contours and warm texture of the living reality. These idealizations, moreover, tend to obscure rather than sharpen our understanding of those significant personalities whose impact on the mind and heart of contemporary India has been tremendous and far-reaching.

This is highly unfortunate—and not only from the narrow standpoint of an abstract ideal of objectivity. For during the past hundred years India has produced in every field men and women who were truly great, not because they possessed an unfailing lucidity of outlook and purpose and a seraphic quality of goodness, but precisely because of the richness and complexity of their humanity. Their experience at once illuminates and reflects the conflicting social and intellectual impulses at work during one of the most confused yet stimulating transitions in Indian history. To all serious social historians and biographers who can resist what Mr Harold Nicolson has aptly called 'the creeping *pietas*', these personalities offer a vast and virgin field for exploration. And among them, perhaps, no personality is more rewarding than that of Mohammed Iqbal.

A great deal has been written about him; a great deal will continue to be written about him; and from all points of view. This is as it should be. As he has confessed in one of his many moments of self-knowledge, his personality is 'a sum of contradictions'. It admits of various interpretations and offers something to everybody. However, and in spite of the ever growing body of literature dealing with his life and work, it is surprising how little we know of him, how meagre is any reliable data about his career, how difficult it is even to establish with authenticity such routine biographical details as his marriages, his relations with his three wives and his children. Much material bearing on his life still remains private property. Though some of his letters to his friends have been published, many still remain locked up in private cupboards and no systematic attempt has been made by his admirers to collect them and present them in a coherent order. The time for a comprehensive biography, therefore, is not yet; and for an outsider to attempt an exhaustive analysis of his work would not only be presumptuous, but undertaking an impossible assignment.

At the same time, however, the handicaps should not be exaggerated. They are undoubtedly exasperating to a degree, but in the ultimate analysis they are, perhaps, less formidable than they appear at first. For the outward details of Iqbal's career are not of such a vital consequence as the unfolding of his spirit and the growth of his mind. He clearly realized this when he told his friends that 'there is no necessity to record these trivial details' in his biography. 'The most important thing,' he added, 'is the exposition of my thought and the tracing of the mental conflict in the evolution of my thought.' Unfortunately, this sound admonition has not been heeded. There has been far too much preoccupation with trivialities which have been charged with significances that they cannot possibly sustain. And as far as his ideas are concerned, the tendency has been to interpret the pattern of his thought in so solemn and schematic a fashion as to obscure the inner conflicts and tensions which made Iqbal and his poetry.

D. H. Lawrence has remarked somewhere that one should mistrust the artist, but trust his art. He might have added that one should mistrust the devotees and admirers of an artist even more than the artist. The proper study of a poet is unquestionably his poetry. Iqbal's poetry, of course, is not autobiographical and personal in the sense in which so much contemporary verse tends to be personal and even exhibitionist. But it does contain that quality of self-revelation which is an essential element in all enduring art. Properly approached, it provides all the necessary clues to an understanding of his personality and the relationship in which he stood to the life of our epoch. Certainly, it is a far more reliable source of information than all the pious glosses and commentaries furnished both during his life and since his death by those who vehemently claim him as their own.

These latter, it should be recorded, were never truly admitted into his deeper confidence. On this point we have the testimony of his own words. For though he had a wide circle of friends, he carried with him throughout his life an almost unbearable burden of solitude which was not wholly self-imposed. It was by no means merely poetic conceit which led him to compose the following lines and instruct that they be inscribed on his tomb:

> When I packed my belongings to depart from this earth
> They all said: 'We knew him well.'
> But truly no one knew this traveller,
> No one knew whence he came, what he said and to whom.

It takes a long time to build mausoleums; bricks and mortar and marble cost money which needs time to collect. Iqbal's mausoleum in Lahore at the time of writing remains still unfinished[1]; and it is not known whether these lines have been inscribed on his tomb. But thirteen years after his death, it is not too early to try to make a tentative and preliminary investigation as to what he said and to whom he said it. That is the main purpose of this introductory essay. I am aware that the aim may well have been too ambitious to be successful. But, there is also a second and less ambitious aim. And that is to record a personal enthusiasm for Iqbal's poetry—an enthusiasm which increases every time I return to it. If, despite manifest defects of interpretation and inadequacies of translation, it succeeds in communicating something of that enthusiasm, this work will, I feel, have justified itself.

Menton                                                                I. S.

---

1. It has been completed since the book was written and published.

# Preface to the Second Edition

Some writers are lucky. They catch the mood of the moment. I cannot claim that kind of luck. At least *The Ardent Pilgrim* could not have been written at a worse time. It was commissioned by the late Cyprian Blagden than in charge of Orient Longman which was at the time a departmental extension to Longmans, Green and Company, in the spring of 1947 over a lunch. The moment was ill chosen for an Introduction to the Life and Work of Mohammed Iqbal. It was just a few months before the partition of India and the creation of Pakistan. The book was largely written in Maison Charles, Route de Gorbio, Menton, in the south of France in the winter of 1948–49. It was published in 1951.

The wounds of partition of the country—and the heart-break it meant for a whole generation of men and women—were still far from healed or even assuaged. Iqbal, whose name was, rightly or wrongly, associated with the authors of Pakistan was not viewed with much favour in India, to put it mildly. In Pakistan, too, in spite of the euphoria at having won a brand-new country 'with no history' as Camus would have said, the more far-sighted people had the feeling that history had taken a wrong turning for which all of us would pay later. Certainly, it was not the dawn, in the words of Faiz Ahmed Faiz, which they had set out to seek 'somewhere beyond the last destination of stars'.

In Pakistan, moreover, this book suffered from a dual disadvantage: first, because it was written by an Indian who was bound to be prejudiced from the start, and, second, because the writer had Sikh antecedents. I learnt from a reliable source, for instance, that even without reading it, the Pakistan High Commission in London placed *The Ardent Pilgrim* on its *Index*. It was only later they discovered that it was not so bad as they had imagined; and that was only because my friend Victor Kiernan in his introduction to his translation of a selection of Iqbal's poems in Urdu, initially published by Kutub (Bombay) and later included in a famous series brought out in London, had said some very generous things about my book. But fortunately—for the publishers, not authors—most books in India, unless they happen to be text books, are brought out in very small editions; and over the years stocks of *The Ardent Pilgrim* have been exhausted and even second-hand copies are rarely seen. Since then some friends have been pressing me that a reprint was overdue.

But there came the rub. To find a publisher is not easy. It needs a good deal of running about to which I am averse. So I did the next best thing. Orient Longman, its original publisher now under Indian ownership and management, were approached, not once but twice—the last time in 1993. But they declined, unless I was prepared to find some institution to subsidize the publication. This seemed an unacceptable condition, believing as all writers do that once the manuscript is completed and made ready for the publisher, the author's job is over for all practical purposes and the book—one is tempted to call it a paper-boat—must sail under its own steam till it finds a haven of refuge.

When *The Ardent Pilgrim* was written, darkness was on the face of the deep, as it were. In other words, very few details of Iqbal's private life were public knowledge. They were all still locked up in the memories of his surviving relations, friends and acquaintances, or in his letters to them and their letters to him. Tracing them would be a lifetime's labour besides being inordinately expensive beyond the resources of any individual. Fortunately, however, over the nearly sixty years since he died, a great deal of biographical material has been unearthed; two very large volumes of his collected letters in Urdu have been published; and there is a constant stream of books about Iqbal—good, bad or indifferent—rolling down the printing presses on both sides of the divide which some have called 'Great' and others say was the greatest act of political vandalism in this century. This has been the case particularly since the centenary of his birth which, for some inexplicable reason, was celebrated in 1977.

Now, therefore, it is possible to delve deeper into his intimate life: his relations with his three wives or other women he loved or was fond of; his alienation from his elder son, Aftab, and the consequent concentration of his affection on his younger son, Jawid; and the relative lack of information about his feelings for his two daughters, Meraj who died young, and Munira who was a child of eight or nine when Iqbal died. There is an additional chapter at the end of the book in which these matters have been tentatively dealt with. If Iqbal emerges from this analysis as a person rather less admirable than the poet in him, it is because, after all, he was human, all too human.

The Mahatma admired Iqbal's poem 'Hindustan Hamara' which was written in his early mood of fervent Indian nationalism because Gandhi felt the same about India. When Jamia Millia Islamiya was founded, he wanted Iqbal to become its Vice-Chancellor. Indeed, an offer was made to him, as Rafiq Zakaria records in his book on Iqbal. But he declined the offer because he had changed his position and no longer felt the same enthusiasm for Indian nationalism. The reasons he gave for his refusal were somewhat disingenuous and became plain enough during the 1930s and onwards. What is significant, however, is that since the late 1950s there has been something of a revolution in Indian sentiment about Iqbal. It is true that Indira Gandhi who, unlike her father, did not know much about Iqbal or his poetry, did not think of issuing a commemorative stamp (which, in these days, are two a penny the world over) to mark the centenary of his birth. But the poetry of Iqbal is engraved on the hearts and minds of many an Indian and today there is a veritable tussle going on between India and Pakistan, each claiming him as its own. Perhaps he belonged to both and it is all to the good that there is this sort of competition in claims. For poetry, as all true art, unites people while politics too often divides them.

However, argument regarding the partition of India will go on as far ahead as one can see. While it would be too simplistic to maintain that Iqbal was a votary of Pakistan, it is true nevertheless that in his lifetime he always differentiated himself from the authors of the Pakistan scheme as it was conceived. I see no reason, therefore, to change what I have said as regards Iqbal's attitude to Pakistan and what it implied. Even in his letter to Jinnah of 21 June 1937—he was less than a year from his death—he harped on 'the only way to a peaceful India is redistribution of the country on the lines of racial, religious and linguistic affinities'. This would have made the task of 'redistribution' infinitely more difficult. For in India political frontiers, until recently, have not been a bar to the movement of people across them and it is hard to find anywhere a racially, linguistically, and religiously homogenous people. He, of course, invoked Lord Lothian in support of his argument and wrote, 'I remember Lord Lothian told me before I left England [at the end of 1932] that my scheme was the only possible solution of the troubles of India, but that it would take 25 years to come.' But it has not happened yet.

Iqbal said a lot of things to a lot of people. He said different things at different times. Whether that is a part of *Kishmiryat*—excess of politeness—one does not know. A spoken word is, however, not a commitment. It is lost in the wind. Different persons, moreover, quote it differently, without the qualifying phrases. But a written word is a commitment, or ought to be. It stands out as a tablet on the sands of time. In so far as Pakistan is concerned, Iqbal has defined his position clearly in a letter he wrote to Edward Thompson on 4 March 1934, from Lahore. He knew that he would be quoted. He said:

> I have just read your review of my book [presumably, the *Reconstruction of Religious Thought in Islam* which had just come out]. It is excellent and I am grateful to you for the very kind things you have said of me. But you have made one mistake which I hasten to point out as I consider it rather serious. You call me protagonist of the scheme called 'Pakistan'. Now Pakistan is not my scheme. The one that I suggested in my address [to the All-India Muslim League at Allahabad in 1930] is the creation of a Muslim Province—i.e. a province having an overwhelming population of Muslims—in the north-west of India. This new province will be, according to my scheme, a part of the proposed Indian Federation. The Pakistan scheme proposes a separate federation of Muslim provinces directly related to England as a separate dominion. This scheme originated in Cambridge. The authors of this scheme believe that our Muslim Round Tables have sacrificed the Muslim nation on the altar of the Hindu or so-called Indian nationalism.

There is good reason to believe that this remained his position till his dying day. All else, including his incidental reference to the Muslims of Bengal in his letter to Jinnah of June 1937, was a passing after-thought.

It only remains now to acknowledge one's debts which are many. I am principally indebted to my friend Victor Kiernan

(Professor Emeritus in Modern History, University of Edinburgh) for lending me photocopies of Iqbal's letters to Edward Thompson, one of which is quoted above, passed on to him by Edward Thompson's son, the late E.P. Thompson, an historian in his own right and an ardent activist of the Anti-Nuclear Movement. Besides, over the six decades we have known each other and discussed Iqbal and India generally, my ideas have become clearer as a result of these discussions, such as they are. I am equally grateful to Dr Fakhir Hussain for his never-failing interest in *The Ardent Pilgrim* and my other writings. He has, moreover, been generous about Iqbal, his knowledge of Urdu and Persian literature being incomparably greater than mine. Finally, I owe a debt of gratitude to the editor of editors of *Sha'ir*, a magazine in Urdu published from Bombay, which brought out a special Iqbal issue in 1988. It ranged far and wide and is absolutely indispensable to anybody working on Iqbal. I have drawn freely on the articles and letters published in it. Long may it prosper although just now conditions are not very favourable for literary and cultural magazines in Urdu where virtue has to be its own reward, especially in Bombay.

Delhi, November 1995                                     I. S.

# Contents

| | | |
|---|---|---|
| I. | Father and Son | 1 |
| II. | The Age of Reason | 9 |
| III. | Cities of the West | 20 |
| IV. | In Search of Faith | 33 |
| V. | The Time of Unveiling | 43 |
| VI. | Message of the East | 59 |
| VII. | A Chapter of Deeds | 73 |
| VIII. | The Dead Sea Fruit | 85 |
| IX. | The Book of Eternity | 97 |
| X. | The Lost Melody | 124 |
| XI. | To Sum Up | 134 |
| XII. | Matters of No Importance? | 147 |
| *A Short Bibliography* | | 173 |
| *Additional Bibliography* | | 174 |
| *Index* | | 175 |

CHAPTER I

Father and Son

First the place: Sialkot is a township on the border of West Punjab and the state of Jammu and Kashmir. Today it has a population of nearly one hundred thousand and forms part of Pakistan. In the seventies of the last century, however, it was not half as populous and nobody had yet heard or dreamt of Pakistan. The town as well as the surrounding country had been annexed by the British after the second Sikh War in 1842; and the conquerors from the North Sea island, with their usual passion for peace and order, had immediately turned it into a garrison headquarters, thus adding yet one more cantonment to the long chain of strongholds, stretching from the mouth of the Ganges to the Indus, with which they intended to protect north-western India against the 'Russian menace' and internal turmoil.

The economic life of the town revolved round the British garrison and the impressive edifice of civilian administration which had followed in due course. Gradually there grew up the commercial and professional classes, merchants, shopkeepers, contractors, lawyers and middle-men whose descendants a hundred years later were to take over power from the British. In the years to come, the place was also to acquire fame throughout India, as the centre of a flourishing sports industry. Tennis rackets and footballs manufactured in Sialkot were soon to make their appearance at Wimbledon and Wembley, thus contributing in no small measure to the prosperity of some of its citizens.

Outwardly, there is little to distinguish Sialkot from any other small town in western Punjab, except perhaps the climate. This, even during the months of great heat, is somewhat less trying owing to the moderating influence of cool breezes from the Sivalik range which forms a blue veil of translucency across the northern horizon. The rainfall is more than average and in the rainy season the countryside around the town is transfigured by the alchemy of water into a luxurious verdure; and the dry river-beds and streams magically come to life and overflow their banks.

The town has a memory. Outside the city limits there is a mound upon which stand the ruins of a fort dating back to the tenth century. Buried deep under this mound are probably relics of an even more distant and tempting Graeco-Buddhist past which some historians identify with Sakala or Sagal. But few among the inhabitants of Sialkot have time for history. Their lives move in the narrow, unemphatic, monotonous rhythms characteristic of small-town ethos, with its parochial pleasures and even more parochial passions, frustrations and pathos.

It was at Sialkot that Mohammed Iqbal was born on 22 February 1873.[1] Originally, his family belonged to Kashmir. Indeed, they were descended from the Sapru branch of Kashmiri Brahmins, a unique ethnic group endowed with great qualities of the mind and heart which has achieved much distinction in diverse fields in recent Indian history. Some time in the seventeenth century Iqbal's forebears had transferred their spiritual allegiance from the Vedas to the Qu'ran, but Iqbal for his part was never altogether able to forget his genealogy and has referred with pride to his Brahminical descent in one of his poems:

> Look well at me, for in India you will not find
> another Man of Brahmin descent who is versed in the
> mysteries of Rüm and Tabriz.

It is not recorded when exactly his ancestors migrated from the valley of Kashmir to the plains. It is safe, however, to surmise that this must have happened during the early part of the eighteenth century, that bitter phase of dynastic upheavals and social anarchy when the Moghul Empire was visibly and rapidly declining towards its fall. The change of habitat does not appear to have had any adverse effect on family fortunes. On the contrary, like most Kashmiris, Iqbal's family prospered rather better in the plains than on higher altitudes; and at the time of Iqbal's birth his father, Sheikh Nur Mohammed, was the owner of a small, moderately profitable tailoring business.

---

1. This date is notional as is the case with all dates in India until quite recently.

Sins of the fathers, according to a proverb, are visited upon their children. So, too, perhaps the virtues of the children are sometimes visited upon their parents; and it is not unusual for fathers of famous sons to shine in the reflected glory of their offsprings' accomplishments. Sheikh Nur Mohammed has undoubtedly suffered from this biographical convention and it is, therefore, not easy to form a clear picture of his personality. However, when due allowance has been made for the inevitable exaggerations and idealizations, he emerges as a man possessed of considerable strength of character and of a quite exceptional piety who devoted much of his time to theological and religious pursuits and cultivated the company of the local Divines.

It should be added, of course, that religion occupied in the life of Muslims of his generation and standing a very important place. It provided a compensation, almost a sense of fulfilment, in a world which was otherwise unsatisfactory, disappointing and, if not hostile, always refractory to human wishes—and, in particular, to Muslim wishes. For the decades that followed the collapse of the Revolt of 1857 were for Muslim India a period of painful disenchantment and emotional crisis whose full measure it is very difficult for us to obtain at this distance. It is true many Hindus, too, had taken part in the movement of 1857; they, too, had felt the heart-break and humiliation of defeat. Yet their anguish was less sharp; it did not possess that quality of personal tragedy which was felt by the Muslims. For all the hopes and aspirations of Muslim India were still bound up with the vanished glory of the Court at Delhi.

This sense of irretrievable loss had created among middle-class Muslims a mood of nostalgic introversion and despair in which the world of religion offered the only possible comfort and consolation. Undoubtedly, as practical men of the world, they realized the need for reaching some sort of a compromise, if not making peace, with the new order that was growing around them under the impact of the industrious North Sea islanders who by now held the whole of India from Cape Comorin to the Khyber Pass under their undisputed sway. But their hearts were disconsolate; and the process of adjustment to the new conditions of life was slow, obstructed by endless psychological reluctances.

The resistance was felt most acutely in the sphere of culture and education. One may have to do business even with an enemy, but accepting his culture, his education, his pattern of spiritual values was another matter altogether. That is how the Muslim mind reasoned; and it is not surprising that for a long time after the 'Mutiny' most Muslims in India who could afford education for their children remained extremely reluctant to send them to the schools established by the British or by the missionaries who had followed the Flag. It certainly speaks a great deal for the common sense of Iqbal's father that, notwithstanding his piety and religious disposition, he had decided to send his eldest son Atta Mohammed, who was Iqbal's senior by some thirteen years, to the local Mission School.

The decision was more difficult to make in Iqbal's case, possibly because having sent one son already to what was for all practical purposes a secular institution, imparting lay education, Sheikh Nur Mohammed felt that he owed it to his religion to send his younger son to the mosque to be trained in the divinities. There were two worlds with which one had to deal; and if one had two sons one ought to share them impartially between both worlds. Iqbal had been sent in the beginning to the Mission School, but when he was studying in the fourth primary class, his father was assailed by doubts as to the wisdom of educating both his sons in a system prejudicial to the True Faith. He almost decided to withdraw Iqbal from the school and send him to the mosque. Before taking this decision, however, he consulted Moulvi Mir Hassan, who taught Arabic and Persian at the school and was an intimate friend of the family.

This was fortunate. For Moulvi Mir Hassan, though himself a man steeped in the old world culture and a scholar of immense erudition in Arabic and Persian, had the good sense to recognize that the old order had no future and that palms other than those of theological disputations had to be won. He advised Sheikh Nur Mohammed to allow Iqbal to continue with his studies, arguing that the boy was destined for 'the School, not the Mosque'. Fortunately for the world of letters Iqbal's father was impressed by this advice and gave up the idea of withdrawing his son from the Mission School.

Places as well as persons mould the mind of the growing child.

In Iqbal's childhood, however, the element of locality seems to have exercised a comparatively negligible influence. We find no echoes in his work of any profound ties with or affection for the place of his birth. During his life he was often to be moved to lyrical expression by the beauty of places in many parts of the world, but he has left us no poetic reminiscences of Sialkot. This may be unusual in a poet who was above all a romantic, but it is not altogether surprising. Sialkot was not the place to which one could become attached or which could stir poetic longings. There were its narrow, congested, insanitary streets and lanes. There were the lives of its inhabitants revolving in even narrower, more congested and insanitary orbits. That was the present; the past was almost forgotten; and the future was the sports industry. There was nothing in all this to be remembered and contemplated in tranquillity, nothing to inspire the imagination, nothing.

But if the physical landscape was uninspiring, this cannot be said of the human landscape. The greatest influence was inevitably the home. Here the atmosphere that prevailed was characteristically patriarchal. Of the women in the family, even of Iqbal's mother, we know little, and are not meant to know anything beyond the fact that she died in 1914 when Iqbal was over forty. In a Muslim home at the time the proper place for a woman was behind the *purdah*; Iqbal himself was to remain a lifelong champion of the veil; and his biographers have discreetly observed the convention. Women in the patriarchal pattern had a function, an important function, but no active and essential part. They ministered to men's wants in various ways; they provided the background, sentimental, decorative, at times protective, but they were seldom allowed to obtrude or assert themselves. Such was the order of things in the household of Iqbal's father as it was to be later in Iqbal's own household. The dominant figure was the Father, endowed with patrician graces and immensely pious. He was the symbol of achievement, but even more important, of authority exercised with a certain stern benevolence. And the symbol imprinted itself indelibly on the mind of the child. As years passed the symbol acquired the quality of a tempting ideal, a standard and a measure for his own personality, a perfection for which he felt he had to strive in his own life.

There were also other eminences in the landscape, less elevated perhaps, but nevertheless impressive. There was Moulvi Mir Hassan.

He was the Arabic teacher at Iqbal's school. Some years later when the status of the school was raised to that of an Intermediate college, Moulvi Mir Hassan was promoted to a lecturership at the college. He was, by all accounts, a remarkable man, vastly learned in the whole domain of Islamic culture. He belonged to that category of scholars and pedagogues, now almost extinct, who, though fated to spend their lives in penury and oblivion, making a precarious living through the ill-paid teaching profession, have during the past hundred years kept the tradition of conscientious oriental scholarship alive by their capacity for taking infinite pains and devotion in a world where these virtues had to be their own reward.

With these academic attainments, Moulvi Mir Hassan combined an even rarer quality of sympathy and understanding of human personality. He was always quick to perceive the spark of true sensibility and intelligence among his pupils and spared himself no trouble to cultivate young promise and offer it friendly advice and encouragement. There is no doubt that he was the person who first detected the symptoms of a sensitive talent in Iqbal. More than detecting these symptoms, he nurtured the child's mind with loving care. He opened, not one, but several windows for Iqbal to look out from; windows which commanded the view of a most magnificent world—the truly rich and strange world of Arabic, Persian and Urdu poetry. He led him step by step through its labyrinths of delight and ecstasy, helped him to scale its precipices of thought and emotion. Under these various stimulations, Iqbal's own mind and heart began to flower, to struggle towards articulation. He began to write verse.

There is nothing strange in an adolescent writing poetry; poetry, indeed, is the prerogative of adolescents all over the world. What Iqbal wrote he first showed to his teacher and guide, Mir Hassan. A less sympathetic teacher might have considered such precocious preoccupations as an indiscretion, if not an impertinence. But Iqbal, unlike Tagore, was to be fortunate in his teachers. Moulvi Mir Hassan gave him encouragement and just the appreciation he needed to persevere. Iqbal persevered. Some of his poems he read publicly at the local symposiums. They could not have been very profound; hardly any of them have survived; but they were admired in local literary circles and they must have possessed some freshness of appeal. Soon, possibly on the advice of Moulvi Mir Hassan, he sent some of his verse to Dagh for correction and criticism.

Dagh was at the time one of the acknowledged masters in Urdu poetry. After the fall of Delhi he had been invited by the Prince of Hyderabad and had settled down in that southern centre of Urdu literature. He had pupils all over India who corresponded with him and sought his opinion of their literary outpourings. Iqbal was a stranger, almost an intruder among Dagh's circle of correspondents. Yet Dagh did not disappoint him: he duly corrected his poems and wrote an encouraging letter. The correspondence course in poetry continued for some time, but before long Dagh wrote back that Iqbal's poetry was in no further need of correction. This must be regarded as a truly remarkable compliment coming as it did from one who was not only a poet of great reputation and an acknowledged master-craftsman, but also a severe and exacting critic by no means given to bestowing cheap praise—who had, in fact, warned all aspiring poets and writers in Urdu in the following words:

> O, Dagh, tell all your friends that it is not a mere matter of play,
> The acquisition of Urdu is a slow and arduous process.

If the earlier appreciation of his teacher, Moulvi Mir Hassan, had given him the necessary stimulus to continue writing verse, Dagh's praise of his efforts finally established his confidence in his imaginative powers. From that moment onwards, though there were to be periods of doubt and hesitancy, Iqbal knew what was his real vocation.

Poets have a reputation of being, if not dull, at least indifferent students. If this is so, then Iqbal was a notable exception. He did not allow his passion for poetry to interfere with the more formal side of his studies. He was, even in the most conventional sense of the term, a 'good' student who took his studies seriously, with the result that at most stages of his academic career he won distinctions and qualified for prizes. He passed his Intermediate from the Mission College and it was decided that he should go to Lahore for further studies. Accordingly, he left for the provincial capital in 1895 where he was to join the Government College which then, as for a long time to come, was the premier institution for higher education, both in the humanities and the sciences, in the Punjab.

Leaving Sialkot was not without its pangs. It meant parting with his friend and teacher, Moulvi Mir Hassan. But there was the excitement of going to a new place. The world was opening out and new and wider horizons were tempting.

CHAPTER II

## The Age of Reason

Lahore in the late nineties of the last century was a very different place from what it was destined to become in the years between the two wars. Much of what is now known as the 'Civil Lines' and the sprawling, untidy, graceless suburbs which house the local bourgeoisie, bearing witness to its power, its prolificness, its wealth and vulgarity, had not yet come into existence. Life for the indigenous population was lived mostly inside the walled city—an immense heap of buildings each one of which appears to communicate with its neighbour, and where streets are like narrow, cavernous defiles. It was overpopulated then, as it is now, unhygienic and malodorous, but not without a certain medieval charm and picturesqueness. Some of its population overflowed outside the limits of the city walls into or around Anarkali—literally the 'bud of pomegranate'—which had already become an important shopping-centre. But no further; for beyond were the bungalows and residences of the members of the ruling race, mysterious, exclusive, and as the enigmatic little box outside each habitation warned the passers-by, permanently 'not at home'.

The Government College where Iqbal was to study for his degree occupied a commanding position, being built on a natural elevation on the road which leads from Anarkali to the Law Courts. An L-shaped building, architecturally it represented a cross between the barrack-room and the Gothic minster, evoking memories of Ruskin in the subtropical latitudes. The well-kept and well-turfed lawns and grounds which surrounded it and insulated it, as it were, from the teeming life of the city, however, invested it with an element of cloistered peace, and even beauty.

A city is more than its physical mass or even those who dwell in it. It has, or should have, a collective personality, a unifying spirit and atmosphere. Lahore in the nineties had such a personality.

It had not yet acquired the arid air of second-rate suburbia, nor the imitative cosmopolitanism, which characterizes it today and which makes it, after New Delhi, the most unlivable metropolis in the Indian subcontinent. It had, of course, fewer amenities: there were no cinemas, no coffee-houses, no restaurant bars where the scions of middle-class families could congregate in the evenings to dance, to drink, to indulge in pseudo-intellectual chatter, and above all to show their smart and gaudy dresses. But if it had not all these modern conveniences, it at least had a culture—a very considerable culture, local, perhaps a trifle provincial, so that Delhi and Lucknow could smile a little condescendingly, but still a culture which was never shallow or vulgar.

Iqbal had no difficulty, though still a student, in being accepted among the literary circles. He was young and endowed with social as well as intellectual graces. And he already enjoyed some reputation as a poet of promise, the coming man if not one already arrived. He became a frequent and familiar figure at the poetic symposiums. These were a regular and distinctive feature of the cultural life in Lahore, as elsewhere in north-western India, in those days. They provided a useful and significant link between the poets and the public. For to these gatherings came not only the initiates, the poets and the critics, but also the laity, the populace. Poetry, indeed, had not yet lost its contact with the people and become a private, almost esoteric cult; it was still a public affair and, in fact, a public pleasure; and something deeply rooted and interfused with life itself. In the world in which Iqbal was to make his debut as a poet the values of the 'cash register' were still by no means supreme: poets might have been as poor, or even poorer than they are today, but they were respected and poetry mattered—mattered unquestionably.

Of the verse which Iqbal wrote during this period of his life a good deal, perhaps far too much, has been preserved in the collection entitled *Bang-i-Dara* (The Caravan Bell). It is partly descriptive, partly lyrical, and often derivative. Apart from the usual influences, those of Urdu and Persian poets, one observes in it other, more distant resonances, and especially, the impact of the English Romantics. There are all the familiar devices of Urdu poetry: its allusions, suggestions, repetitions and reticences. But it also contains something more: a boldness of image and metaphor, and above all, a certain argumentativeness, indicating a mental inquietude, a restlessness born of the urge to break through the limitations of his medium. And it is not unreasonable to claim that Iqbal, even at this stage of his career, was trying not merely to sing, but to affirm something, to charge his verse with the sharp polarities of ideas.

It is not surprising that his poems evoked ardent admiration as well as hostile criticism. More important, perhaps, than this strong spirit of partisanship, they succeeded in winning the approval of some of the more discerning critics and fellow-craftsmen. It is recorded, for example, that at one of the symposiums Mirza Arshad of Gurgaon, who commanded great respect as a poet, burst out into ecstatic praise when he heard Iqbal recite the following couplet:

> Divine Grace has gathered them
> as though they were pearls,
> those drops which were
> the drawn-out essence of my remorse.

Youth is golden and youth is ardent. And Iqbal was possessed of a temperament which was nothing if not ardent. His youthful years, therefore, could not but be turbulent. He was the centre of much admiration, even hero-worship by a group of his contemporaries. Legends are bound to grow round such a personality; and legends have grown. There are stories of adolescent passions, of daring escapades, of visits during the twilight hours to a well-known quarter in Lahore where on their dimly-lit balconies overlooking narrow lanes, the priestesses of Venus preside over intimate festivals of fire, ministering to their devotees for a consideration not only the absolution of the flesh, but of the soul as well. Whether these stories are true or not we shall never know for certain. Some of them are obviously and wholly apocryphal; others less so. But apocryphal or not, they do to some degree throw light on what may well be described as the process of Iqbal's *education sentimentale*. It is safe to suggest that this process was not entirely of a Platonic character; and that explains why his early verse manages at times to communicate the tension of experienced emotion and not merely the vapourings of a disembodied fancy.

Iqbal's student days in Lahore coincided with an important phase in the evolution of modern India and particularly Muslim India. It may be said with some justice that the Muslim intelligentsia in India has gone through all those stages of development which its Hindu counterpart has known—only with a time-lag. It was Raja

Rammohan Roy who initiated the movement of reform and rationalization of Hindu thought by founding the Brahmo Samaj in the early decades of the nineteenth century. Almost half a century later Sir Saiyed Ahmed Khan was to launch the Aligarh Movement which, though different in some of its superficial aspects, was in its inner purpose and content essentially identical with the movement started by the Hindu reformer.

The Aligarh Movement, which found its material expression in the establishment of the Aligarh College, was inevitably motivated by a complex set of impulses. It claimed to be at once a movement of reform and revival of Islamic culture, but its proclaimed aims were not necessarily its real aims. In its origin, it was primarily rooted in the economic necessities of the Muslim middle class. Sir Saiyed's basic aim was to free his community from that mood of unavailing despair and nostalgic fatalism into which it had lapsed after the defeat of 1857, and draw it into the full tide of new times. He recognized this to be an imperative need, especially in view of the fact that the Hindus, who were not inhibited by any such complexes, were taking full advantage of the educational facilities provided by the British, and thus virtually monopolizing whatever crumbs of political and economic advantage that were being offered to Indians. Muslims had to come to terms with the present; they could not afford to lie in cold obstruction and rot; and it was the main ambition of Sir Saiyed and his associates to enable their co-religionists to overcome the intellectual, psychological and metaphysical inhibitions which prevented them from accepting the present.

These economic urgencies, of course, had their repercussions in other spheres—in letters, in philosophy, even in theology. The Aligarh Movement produced a brilliant group of writers, historians, and poets among whom the most famous was Altaf Husain Hali of Panipat whose best known long poem, the *Musaddas*, may be regarded as the poetic argument for the Aligarh Movement, articulating as it does the nascent spirit of pragmatic rationalism which that movement embodied.

By the nineties of the last century the Aligarh Movement had gathered immense momentum. Originating, in the first instance, in the United Provinces it had become an all-India movement with enthusiastic supporters everywhere, despite some opposition from the Muslim orthodoxy. Its influence had reached the capital of the

Land of Five Rivers, Lahore. There was an active branch of the Anjuman-i-Himayat-i-Islam (Society for the Aid of Islam) in the city, the purpose of which was to promote by every possible means the cultural, educational and social interests of the Muslims.

Iqbal, who had a highly receptive mind, had come under the influence of the Aligarh spirit. He took a keen interest in the work of the Anjuman, an interest which was to prove lifelong and abiding. He attended its various public functions and read poems which were intended to awaken the interest of the Muslim community in its great cultural heritage. At the annual session of this Society in 1899 he was to recite a poem entitled 'Nala-i-Yatim'—(Orphan's Cry)—which was to win him a much wider public than he had known so far. It is not in itself a remarkable work by any critical standards; it represents an essay in that plaintive and pathetic mode which often recurs in his early verse; but it had a remarkable response. It moved the bowels of compassion of his audience, most of whom were Muslims, to the very depths; many people wept, we are told; and later, when the meeting was over, enthusiastic admirers nearly mobbed the poet.

The incident, though apparently trivial, is not without significance and invites speculation. Was it merely an example of the sentimentality which comes easily to Punjabi audiences? Possibly. But a more rational explanation is, perhaps, to be found in the fact that the poem struck a note of emotional recognition, a chord of psychological identification, among Iqbal's Muslim listeners. In the cry of the orphan they read their own heart's cry: they too had long felt forlorn and abandoned and this element was to be a compulsive factor in moulding the psychology of Indian Muslims in the years to come. It was to produce in them a sense of grievance, a permanent alienation complex.

However, the Aligarh Movement was not the only intellectual force at work during this, the formative period in Iqbal's life. There were other impulses and influences. There was the spirit of Indian nationalism. The Indian National Congress had been founded in 1885; it had received some official patronage and encouragement in the beginning; but it had soon outgrown the bounds which its early official patrons had set for its activities. It was, of course, still a respectable organization, functioning strictly within constitutional limits, and confining its appeal wholly to the middle and professional classes. Nevertheless, it had stimulated strong nationalist sentiments and impulses.

The Aligarh Movement, it is true, was not altogether sympathetic to the concept of all-India nationalism. Its founder, Sir Saiyed Ahmed Khan, made no secret of his suspicions of, if not active hostility to, the Indian National Congress. The organization was not loyal enough to the temporal power for his liking. He had early come to the conclusion that the Muslim community had suffered because it had got on the wrong side of the ruling power and was suspected by its representatives of disloyalty. He wanted his co-religionists to prove by their acts and words that they were loyal to the British, totally and unreservedly loyal. For loyalty, he maintained, was the best policy; and had discovered even metaphysical and Qu'ranic sanctions for this argument. What is more, already incipient symptoms of that economic rivalry between the two major communities of India—which was to bear so strange and bitter a fruit in the future—were beginning to manifest themselves. Nevertheless, Muslim India was not yet entirely unresponsive to the spirit of nationalism. As yet, what may be described as Muslim nationalism did not run counter to the mainstream of Indian nationalism, but in a direction parallel with it; and Muslim youth in particular, participated fully in the national movement.

Iqbal was one of those who found the appeal of the patriotic idea irresistible. The great and golden past of India, transmuted by distance in time and space into the very perfection of enchantment, stirred his youthful imagination. The beauty of the Indian landscape, the loveliness of the dawn, the brief, unearthly apocalypse of twilight, the magic of the sickle moon, rains, the Himalayas—all these moved him to passionate song. More than that, he wrote poems, obviously propagandist in purpose, but in which the propagandist argument is sustained by a magnificent lyricism. It was during these years that he wrote the poem called 'New Temple' in which he accuses the Brahmin priest that he has learned 'the hatred of his kindred from the idols' and goes on to say that the preacher in the mosque, too, has been taught 'conflict and war by his God'; and he ends on a note of vehement and patriotic fraternalism:

>   Come, let us yet once more
>   lift the veil of estrangement,

unite those who have parted,
remove all traces of duality.

This habitation of the heart
which for so long has remained desolate,
here in this land
let us raise a new temple.

Let our place of pilgrimage
be higher than all the pilgrimages of the world,
let us raise its pinnacle
to the very edge of heavens.

It was also about this time that he wrote his 'Song of the Indian Children' and the even better known 'Hamara Hindustan'—Our India. The latter remains to this day the best patriotic poem written by any Indian poet in modern times. It comes nearest, in fact, to a truly non-communal, national anthem for India.

His poems on patriotic as well as Islamic themes were bound to enhance his reputation not only among the narrow coterie of intellectuals in Lahore where he lived, but among the Urdu-speaking people all over India. Few poets in recent Indian history have added more to the repertory of popular songs than Iqbal.

Poetry was bringing Iqbal well-merited popularity, but one cannot live by popularity alone. Poetry was regarded as a vocation, an exalted vocation, but too exalted to be paid for; and Iqbal, who was by now in his middle-twenties, had to make a living. He had graduated from the Government College, Lahore, winning distinction in English Literature and Arabic and qualifying for a scholarship. He took his MA in Philosophy from the same college in 1899 and once again distinguished himself by winning a gold medal. Soon after, he was appointed as a Reader in Arabic at the Oriental College, Lahore. Later, he was transferred from the Oriental College to Government College across the road where he had studied.

However, these years at Lahore were important for Iqbal, not so much for the academic distinctions that he won, or even the poetic reputation that he established, as for a number of friendships which he formed. One of these was with Thomas (later Sir Thomas)

Arnold who had been his teacher at the Government College. This was to prove to be a very profound and lasting relationship, and Iqbal has more than once acknowledged his debt to Arnold in his poetry—one of his most moving early poems, written in an elegiac vein, was composed on the occasion of Arnold's departure from India.

Thomas Arnold had once taught at Aligarh. Later he joined the Indian Educational Service and came to Lahore. It may be said, even at the risk of being digressive, that of all the complicated, top-heavy, and expensive apparatus of administration which the British had set up during their occupation of India, the Indian Educational Service was the one service which could claim to have justified the Indian money that was spent on it. The Army played polo, drank whisky, slept or engaged in manoeuvres and punitive expeditions on the North-West Frontier. The Police looked after revolutionaries of various descriptions. The Indian Civil Service—the Convenanted Service whose members claimed to be 'heaven-born'—dispensed justice, collected revenue, and qualified for titles and pensions which ran into four figures, but it seldom emerged from its narrow, water-tight world of officialdom to make contact with the life of India. The Medical Service looked after the physical well-being of the Civil Service, the Police and the Army. But it was different for the Britishers in the Education Service. All of them were by no means interested in their work, but quite a few were. What is more, their job was such that they could not all the time maintain the aloof correctness of the Superior Race. They had to meet the students, in the class-room, if nowhere else. They thus came into contact with the mind of young India—eager, responsive, highly impressionable and, let it be added without undue modesty, often possessed of a keen intellect and passionately interested in the world of ideas. Those among the British educationalists who happened to be men of sympathy and sensibility—and there were a considerable number of these—could not help being impressed by their pupils and they did what they could to rescue their students from the stultifying effect of an educational system specially designed to kill all mental initiative and produce mediocrities.

Arnold was one such educationalist to whom India owes a debt of gratitude. Of a highly cultured and sensitive nature, he gave of his best to his students. In Iqbal he immediately recognized an unusual talent and intellectual potentiality. He befriended him, encouraged him in his pursuits, and gave him sympathy so essential to a growing mind—and gave it in abundant measure. If Moulvi Mir Hassan had opened for Iqbal the world of Eastern thought and poetry through the medium of Persian, Arabic and Urdu, Arnold completed the process of education. He opened for Iqbal the world of Western thought and literature and the vast riches of its achievements in the humanities. The two discoveries were complementary. Iqbal was always a keen explorer of the countries of the mind and, with Arnold's guidance, he was soon at home in this newly discovered world of the spirit.

Arnold was helpful to Iqbal in other, still more practical ways. In India then, as now, there is only one access to governmental benefices—influence of powerfully placed individuals. It is safe to assume that Arnold's interest in Iqbal was influential in getting for him the post of Reader in Arabic at the Oriental College and later that of a lecturer in English at the Government College. And there is little doubt that it was Arnold who finally persuaded Iqbal to go for higher studies to Europe.

Iqbal taught for some six years in the two institutions we have mentioned. These were fruitful and productive years, a period of vigorous rationalism and steady intellectual growth. He wrote a great deal of poetry during this period. Not all is of equal merit. Some of the poems are conventional, others obviously derivative, but there are also utterances of a crystalline beauty. Many influences were at work, some local and contemporary, others from afar. The dominant influences were the Sufi poets of Persia and the English Romantics. The former gave his poetry intellectual and emotional depth; from the latter he derived his love of nature and most of the descriptive poems must be attributed to the impact of the Romantic Movement.

His verse appeared in many journals, but most of it in the periodical *Makhzan* which was started by his friend and admirer, Sheikh Abdul Qadir. Some of the poems of this period were written specially for *Makhzan*. Inspiration in these days was never lacking and poetry came to Iqbal easily, perhaps too easily. In the room where he slept, he kept a notebook and pencil at hand so that he could take down any verses that might come to him at night.

Sometimes he would dictate the poem to any friend who happened to be visiting him. Sheikh Abdul Qadir has related how once he went to Iqbal to ask him to write a poem for *Makhzan*. It was late in the evening and Iqbal asked him to take down the poem and began composing extempore. He went on dictating the whole night and it was not until the morning that the poem was completed.

We get few glimpses of his life during these years. For Iqbal has not been fortunate in his biographers. His old servant Ali Bakhash has recounted an episode in the Urdu journal *Shiraza* which throws interesting light on Iqbal's extraordinary obliviousness to physical danger. It happened during the earthquake which worked enormous havoc at Kangra and more or less affected the whole of the Punjab. 'The earthquake,' says Ali Bakhash, 'was like God's judgement. First, the doors began to rattle; then the earth heaved as though the world was coming to an end. I was panic-stricken and kept running up and down the stairs. Many houses in the two were collapsing and all around there was commotion. But Sheikh Sahib (meaning Iqbal) was lying on his bed in his room and reading a book. He did not stir from his bed. Only, when he saw me in panic, he raised his eyes from the book he was reading and said: "Ali Bakhash, don't keep running up and down like this. Go and stand under the stairs." And once again he returned to his book as though nothing was happening.'

The routine of his life was simple. He was always an early riser and has even written a poem which begins:

> Though the winter air was sharp like the sword,
> I could not give up the habit of early-rising, even in
>                                the West.

From his father he had imbibed the habit of attending to his prayers regularly and every morning he rose at dawn to say his prayers. Often, after his prayers, he spent some time reading aloud from the Qu'ran. This pious regime was followed by physical exercises. By the time they were completed it was time to go to the college. He generally went to work before having had his breakfast and had his main meal of the day about one o'clock on his return from the college. In the evening he sometimes drank tea—with salt, not sugar. For a poet who has written so lyrically and with such infectious abandon in his verse of the delights of wine and the charms of the cup-bearer, of nocturnal revels in the tavern and the Bacchic ecstasy, this must appear a singularly ascetic and unexciting regime. But, then, perhaps imagined wines are always sweeter, more luscious and intoxicating than any that were ever fermented from the juice of the crushed grape.

Soon, of course, Iqbal was to taste other than metaphorical wines. Arnold had completed his term of employment and gone back to England. He had been advising Iqbal to visit Europe and at last Iqbal had agreed. He sailed for England in 1905.

CHAPTER III

## Cities of the West

Ever since the beginning of the nineteenth century, the Indian intelligentsia has looked towards the West; looked sometimes openly and frankly, sometimes furtively and with secret longing as at a forbidden land of promise. And in the West it is England and her universities which have symbolized for the Indian middle class a kind of intellectual and cultural Mecca, the ultimate source of all that is good and true and beautiful. Sons and, somewhat more rarely, daughters of well-to-do Indians were sooner or later sent to England to complete their education and to acquaint themselves with the ways of life of the ruling race in whose hands an inscrutable Providence had placed the destiny of India. These visits involved expense, sometimes real sacrifices, and often very grave doubts as to the moral well-being of their progenies on the part of the parents. For the visiting pilgrims, old or young, it involved considerable physical discomfort, some psychological upsets, and not infrequently, fall from grace. But the pilgrimage was worth it. For in its motives it was essentially economic rather than Platonic. English education improved the worldly prospects of those who could afford it; it raised their value in the higher and restricted labour market—and even in the wider marriage market. At least this was the situation till the end of the First World War when the inflation started.

So, for one reason or another, they all made their pilgrimage—Raja Rammohan Roy, Sir Saiyed Ahmed Khan, Rabindranath Tagore, Mohandas Karmchand Gandhi and Jawaharlal Nehru, to mention the most eminent. Iqbal when he left for England was, therefore, only maintaining a tradition. But there is a difference to be noted. Of the visits of most other eminent Indians we have some detailed records in the form either of their own personal reminiscences or those of their friends; and these are interesting, often illuminating documents. We know, for instance, of Raja Rammohan Roy's discussions with the British Unitarians and Parliamentarians. Sir Saiyed Ahmed Khan in his delightful letters from Europe has described his excitement in London and his indignation in Paris when, at Versailles, he was confronted with a painting depicting the capture by the French of the harem of Abdul Kadir in various stages of abandon in the battle of Algiers. Rabindranath Tagore has written with gentle irony of his musical ministrations for the benefit of a disconsolate Anglo-Indian widow living somewhere in the Home Counties. Mahatma Gandhi has shared with us his moral tribulations and experiments in vegetarianism in London. The Old School Tie flutters across many pages of Jawaharlal Nehru's sensitive and sentimental prose. But Iqbal has not reminisced. He has been very uncommunicative regarding his experience in the West, except for an enigmatic reference in one of his poems suggesting that he entertained a soft corner in his heart for England and Germany, which may or may not have been due to someone's beautiful blue eyes. And this is a pity.

It is an even greater pity that his friend and contemporary, Sheikh Abdul Qadir who was with him during his stay in the West, has hardly been more communicative. He might have been Iqbal's Boswell, might have been, but decided not to be. It is true he has furnished us with some information regarding Iqbal's life in Europe, but it deals with comparatively trivial details, is cursory, and very rarely enlightening. On matters which might have helped posterity to reconstruct the emotional and spiritual development which Iqbal went through during these years, Sheikh Abdul Qadir has observed a silence which is as discreet as it is exasperating.

We are thus left with large blanks which have to be filled in through guesswork. We can and must, of course, try to verify our guesses against the testimony of his work, try to scrutinize it for some moments of self-revelation and excursions into personal reminiscences. But this is a difficult assignment. How difficult, everyone who is familiar with the highly stylized and conventionalized modes and patterns of Persian and Urdu poetry must be aware. For these conventions and stylizations are extraordinarily deceptive. Outwardly, most Urdu and Persian poetry appears to have the character of almost confessional statement and the poets, as it were, wear their hearts on their sleeves.

But this frankness is an illusion and a mirage. As soon as we try to get hold of some solid strand of individual experience which would lead us to the inner recesses of a man's soul, we immediately come up against veil after veil of reticences, depth after depth of an impenetrable reserve; we feel we are shut out by an invisible wall of blinding opaqueness, excluded from any true intimacy; and all our efforts to reach the core of a poet's personality are frustrated by misleading avowals which are always infinitely amiable and infinitely evasive.

This is so with Iqbal who is never more impersonal than when he seems to be on the personal level. He was a man of vast reserve, of monumental reticence. We can, therefore, do no more than give the bare outline of these significant years in his life. That they were significant can be stated with some certainty. It was during this period that there began that process of change and reorientation which was completely to transform his outlook, his social and political philosophy, his whole personality. It is equally certain that he went through some kind of a spiritual crisis during this period. Sheikh Abdul Qadir has hinted at it by recording that at one stage during his stay in Europe he nearly decided to give up writing poetry altogether and to devote himself to some more tangible and active pursuits. He was persuaded against this fatal decision only by the pressure of Sheikh Abdul Qadir's advice and that of Arnold's. But what were the reasons of this crisis and how precisely did the changes in his outlook and personality come about, we shall never know except in a very superficial way.

Outwardly, his three years spent in the West were uneventful and undramatic. But, then, outwardly, the whole course of his life can hardly be claimed to have been full of drama and incident. Yet it is not only the outwardly dramatic and eventful which shape human personality. There are other adventures, adventures of the mind which, though they often pass unnoticed, exercise a decisive influence on man's destiny. It is on these deeper levels of consciousness that we have to look for the impacts which were to determine the movement of his thought. Iqbal was pre-eminently a man of ideas, rather than deeds; and it is ideas rather than events which constitute the warp and woof of the fabric of his experience. This is not to say that he lived a life of complete subjectivity or that external events did not affect him. It is merely to suggest that even these external events affected him most when they had been translated to the realm of thought. It is on that plane, therefore, that for the most part any narrative of his life has to move.

Iqbal went to Trinity College at Cambridge to study Philosophy. The choice of the subject was fortunate. It brought him into contact with two leading figures in the world of philosophy in England at the time—Professors McTaggart and James Ward. McTaggart was at the time giving a course of lectures on Kant and Hegel, and Iqbal studied under his direction. James Ward, who is today almost forgotten outside academic circles, had made an important contribution to Philosophy in his *Naturalism and Agnosticism*. Iqbal all his life valued McTaggart's friendship, though his influence on his own thought was less marked than that of Ward whose ideas left a much more abiding impress on Iqbal's mind—so that Professor M. M. Sharif in an article in the *Islamic Culture* has gone so far as to describe Iqbal as 'Ward's disciple'.

Iqbal's stay in Cambridge coincided with an interesting phase in the history of English thought. It was a period of neo-Hegelian ascendancy, of a return to idealism in Philosophy. The Victorian Age had been an age, notwithstanding its strait-laced morality, of unbridled materialism, of scientific advances and prosperity, of imperialist consolidation of Britain's world position. In the sphere of thought there was Herbert Spencer's positivism, Darwin's theories of evolution, and Huxley's scepticism which went under the more respectable name of Agnosticism. Towards the end of this epoch, however, a reaction had set in. People were seeking solace in metaphysics and wanted idealistic justifications for a world in which ordinary human intercourse was all on the basis of the cash register. Thus began, on the one hand, the interest in Eastern mysticism and religion; and, on the other, a revival of enthusiasm for Germany's idealistic philosophers.

Among the latter, Hegel's appeal was particularly strong. It is true Karl Marx had neatly and once for all 'put Hegel on his feet'. But among the British academic philosophers, with the characteristically British passion for the oblique vision, Hegel was still preferred, so to speak, on his head. In other words, it was not so much the Hegelian method of interpreting reality as his airy abstractions and metaphysics which attracted them. There had thus grown up in England a very considerable body of thought which in one way or another was inspired by Hegelian ideas. Associated with this trend were men of such undisputed eminence in the philosophic world as Green, Bradley, Bosanquet and McTaggart himself of whom Iqbal was to say that he stood in the same relation to Hegel as 'Leibnitz was to Spinoza'.

It is fairly certain that Iqbal during this phase of his career came under the spell of Hegelian ideas. Later in his life he was to turn his back on Hegel as, indeed, on the whole body of Western idealistic thought—from Plato downwards. But it is not easy to outgrow the enchantments of one's youth and there is no doubt that Iqbal, even when he was most strongly reacting against his early philosophic loves, could not altogether succeed in repudiating their fascination for him.

There were other attractions besides Hegel. There was Bergson. Bergson's theories of time and of the 'pure duration', which is beyond time, appealed to Iqbal. In a very different, and perhaps more decisive way, Nietzsche's philosophy of the Superman with its passionate insistence on the development of the human ego to its uttermost limit—and, indeed, beyond that limit—profoundly impressed Iqbal.

It would, however, be misleading to give the impression that Iqbal during these years was falling into the habit of philosophic mendicancy and begging and borrowing ideas wherever he could find them. A more accurate suggestion would be that contact with these ideas provided a necessary stimulus to the growth of his own mind; these ideas acted as some kind of catalytic agents in the process without necessarily always entering into it. Iqbal's own philosophic position at this stage, of course, was by no means very definite. In so far as he was under any definite influence, it was of the vague, but highly satisfying, pantheistic concepts of the Sufi poets of Persia. He had not yet transferred his allegiance from the rich wines of Shiraz to the more austere vintage of Tabriz. Hafiz and not Rumi was still his spiritual inspiration. If anything, contact with the famous Cambridge scholar of Persian, Professor E. G. Browne—whose two volumes of *A Literary History of Persia* remain to this day the most authoritative work in English on the subject—had confirmed Iqbal's own poetic predilections. At the same time, however, it is not unlikely that underneath the surface other immortal longings were beginning to take shape. For even as early as 1903 Iqbal had written to one of his friends expressing his dissatisfaction with his own lyrical mode of expression in these words:

> For a long time I have been yearning to write in the manner of Milton (*Paradise Lost*, etc.) and the time for that seems to be fast approaching, because in these days there is hardly a moment, when I am not thinking seriously of this. I have been nurturing this wish for the past five or six years, but the creative pangs have never been so acute as now.

However, these yearnings were still struggling in vain for an outlet. The creative pangs had to go on for several years longer before Iqbal could realize his purpose. The shell of the old self had still not burst and the current of his poetic inspiration still flowed through the lush growth of the fertile pastures of Sufi Persia.

There was all the same one important and positive result of these creative pangs. Until his visit to Europe Iqbal had written verse almost wholly in Urdu. There were moments when he even thought of devoting his whole life to the perfection of this language. In one of his poems he had observed: 'This lamp yearns for the heart-burning of some ardent moth;' and by that lamp he had meant the Urdu language. But now in London he for the first time turned to Persian as a medium of poetic expression.

Sheikh Abdul Qadir has related how it all began. At a party Iqbal was asked by somebody whether he ever wrote verse in Persian. He replied that he had occasionally written a verse or two, but never a whole poem. That evening, on returning to his lodgings from the party, he tried to compose in Persian and by the morning he had written two complete poems. From then on, though he was still to write a great deal of Urdu verse, he was to adopt Persian as the principal vehicle of his thought and poetry.

It is easy to see the reasons for Iqbal's preference for Persian as a medium of expression. It is a language rich in associations; sweet and delicate to a degree that has won for it the title of 'French of the Middle East'; and it possesses a vast and varied vocabulary adequate to the expression of the most complex, the most abstract and difficult nuances of thought and emotion. For Iqbal, struggling to articulate the deeper yearnings of his soul, Persian had everything that he could wish for. Urdu had graces; Urdu had a manner; but in the world of languages it was a newcomer, some almost called it a parvenu, with a history less than five hundred years old as against Persian's two thousand years and more. Its amenities were necessarily limited, even exasperatingly so. For Iqbal the choice of Persian, therefore represented a choice of the line of least resistance; it simplified his problems enormously as a poet, or at least seemed to simplify them.

But the line of least resistance is, in the long-term perspective, often the line of worst resistance. It can prove fatal. Has it proved so in Iqbal's case? This is a difficult question to answer, for it is a very controversial question. At any rate, one thing is certain. Had Iqbal continued to place the burnt offerings of his heart at the altar of Urdu, had he continued to offer his poetic breast (if we may coin the phrase) for the 'locks of Urdu' to rest upon, as he once promised, there is no question that he would have made a tremendous contribution to the development of that language as a modern and comprehensive medium of expression. His contribution, great as it is now, would have been even greater, comparable to that of Tagore to Bengali language and literature. But Iqbal proved wanting in constancy. He found the attractions of Persian more tempting and turned his attentions to this outlandish, but in India never an alien, literary love.

The loss that this meant to Urdu is beyond measure. But can it be claimed that the gain of Persian was commensurate with the loss suffered by Urdu? That is another question bound up with a very important literary controversy. Highly partisan views have been expressed on the issue by both sides. There is little doubt that contemporary Persian critics do not regard Iqbal's Persian poetry as possessing any outstanding merit; some of them have publicly described him as a more or less 'local poet'. He does not figure in anthologies of modern Persian poetry. Dr Sachchidananda Sinha in his 'Iqbal: The Poet and His Message'—a bulky essay in amiable and somewhat irritatingly digressive denigration—has collected a great deal of evidence to support this view.[1]

---

[1] During the past two years a more direct acquaintance with Iqbal's Persian poetry has brought about a change in this uninformed view among the Iranian intelligentsia. Recently several articles have been published in Persian journals on Iqbal's work; and Mujtaba Minovi, a well-known Iranian writer, has written a long and appreciative monograph on Iqbal's Persian poetry entitled *Iqbal, Persian Poet of Pakistan*, even though Pakistan was born nine years after the death of Iqbal.

Nevertheless, one would do well to take these pharisaical judgements with a considerable measure of reserve. In part they are based on grounds which have little to do with any literary values, being dictated by a very subtle form of xenophobia from which even intellectuals are not immune; in part the underestimation of the worth of Iqbal's work in Persian arises from the influence of the 'purist' movement in modern Persian letters—a movement which tends to underestimate, if not skip over, the Islamic phase of Persian literature, and in particular, of the Arabic influences in it.

In any event, it must be stated, that there is a very important body of what can best be described an Indo-Persian poetry and literature just as in the past hundred and fifty years there has grown up an Indo-Anglian literature. This may not find the same unqualified acceptance in Iran as it does in India, but that is not really relevant. What is relevant is that it will remain a part of the literary heritage of India, whatever Teheran may think, and to this tradition Iqbal has added one of the richest chapters.

From England Iqbal went for a time to Germany on Arnold's advice. He studied at the University of Munich as a research student and also attended a course at Heidelberg. The visit to Germany was important for other than purely academic reasons. It provided Iqbal with an opportunity to have a more direct and intimate access to German Philosophy and Literature. He drank from this source of heady wines deeply, perhaps a trifle indiscriminately. Cambridge had only been an introduction to a new country; now the whole landscape lay open to him. He explored it with the zest which was always characteristic of him where horizons of the human mind were concerned. Hegel was now only one summit among many: there was Kant, there was Schopenhauer, there was Goethe—and Schiller. Each height was more tempting than the other.

But life was not all being lived on an exalted level of philosophic intensity. It had its lighter side. At least at Heidelberg, we learn, Iqbal began his academic career with an amusing encounter with Frauleins Wegenast, Senechal and Schat. Iqbal had always been what in modern political terminology might be called an anti-feminist. His father's patriarchal concepts had left an abiding impression on his mind. He did not believe that women had any place in the world of active social life. Their proper place, according to him, was the home, not the university and certainly not the office, or the factory. He believed in purdah, though he may have only meant purdah of the heart rather than that worn across the face. He always recoiled from what he considered lack of modesty of modern womanhood. He has written some satirical verses, in the manner of Akbar of Allahabad, on the subject. One of them, for example, says:

> It is quite unjust for the college students to get
>                 annoyed with the Preacher,
> For he is not really an advocate of *Purdah*.
> Was it not Yesterday that he declared quite frankly
>                 in his sermon:
> What is the point of *Purdah* when men themselves
>                 have become womanly?

With these anti-modern views, it is well to imagine his surprise when he discovered that—it had been arranged with poetic justice—that he was to study language, poetry and philosophy at Heidelberg under three professors all of whom were women. Attia Begum has described their first interview with Iqbal in an article: 'His teachers in Heidelberg were three young women professors—Frauleins Wegenast, Senechal and Schat. In the first informal interview in the garden Iqbal's expression was sarcastic and almost sinister. Just three well-groomed young women: he was not going to consider them seriously. A sharp rejoinder, however, soon brought him round. The sarcasm soon changed to serious attention as through the academic training of the clever young women professors he was to acquire his Ph.D. in a very short time.'

His doctorate, which he got from Munich, was on the strength of his thesis which has since appeared under the title: *The Development of Metaphysics in Persia*. It is a conscientious piece of research work, as practically everything that he wrote in prose was conscientious. But it is somewhat unsatisfying. It leaves the reader with the impression of something that he can neither accept as serious work nor reject as something trivial and unworthy of attention. For a research thesis its scope is too wide; and for an original and interpretative study of the subject it seems too sketchy, too descriptive. It dates badly; and Iqbal himself acknowledged this. In a note to its translation in Urdu written in 1928 he admitted that very little of the book 'is above criticism'.

There was yet another direction in which Iqbal's outlook was undergoing crucial change: his social and political ideas were being profoundly modified by his experience in Europe. During his early years in Lahore he had been affected by the strong winds of Indian nationalism. This influence, it is true, ran parallel to his more fundamental interest in Islamic revivalism, but it was a potent force in moulding the pattern of his mind. His stay in Europe, however, was to raise in his mind serious doubts and misgivings as to the value of certain concepts which earlier he had been inclined to accept with a light-hearted enthusiasm.

Nationalism was one of these concepts. Europe, during the decade that preceded the First World War, revealed to the detached observer the limitations, and indeed, the dangers inherent in the doctrine of political nationalism. The rivalries and conflicts between the European powers—rivalries and conflicts which arose from nationalistic and imperialistic greed—were coming to a head and the whole continent was trembling on the verge of a catastrophe. Few people in Europe may have realized at the time that the disaster was so near. In England, at any rate, the after-glow of Victorian prosperity had lingered on into the Edwardian age with its mock rococo graces and gaiety. There may have been rumblings of thunder on the continent where the Balkans were always a powder magazine about to explode, but those were far-off countries and regions about which the British people knew nothing and did not even care to know anything. The sun was still shining without interruption on the British Empire; the British Navy still enjoyed undisputed sovereignty over the waves of all the world's seas and oceans; and the frontiers of England were still on the Channel, not the Rhine or the Elbe.

But Iqbal was not blessed with the British capacity for self-deception and insouciance. He had been in Germany and he had observed the mood there, particularly among the youth. Apart from this local factor, with a clairvoyance which was characteristic of him, he—like Tagore much later—foresaw that nationalism, especially when allied with an aggressive, acquisitive and destructive doctrine of imperialism, could only have one issue—war. He read the signs on the horizon, read them correctly, and sounded a note of warning:

> O, dwellers of the cities of the West,
> This habitation of God is not a shop,
> and that which you regard as true coin,
> will prove to be only a counterfeit.
> Your civilization will commit suicide
> with its own sword.
> For, remember, a nest built on a fragile bough,
> can never endure.

But few in Europe could read the language in which this warning from the East had been uttered; hardly anyone knew of the poet who had uttered it; and it was lost on the wind.

Iqbal found nationalism wanting and inadequate as a political and social philosophy for reasons other than its practical results and the fact that it produced the dead sea fruit of war and international conflict. He found it unsatisfactory for deeper emotional and spiritual reasons. On closer examination the concept of nationalism appeared to be a continuation, even a throw-back, to the tribal mentality. To judge a man's identity by reference to the territorial accident of his birth was demonstrably to reduce the essential worth of human personality. It was in its way as lowering to human dignity, as humiliating, as the barbarous habit of defining a man's worth in terms of the colour of his skin or the shape of his nose.

The problems raised by these doubts and misgivings were fundamental. They demanded fundamental solutions. For if nationalism as a basis for polity was inadequate and unsatisfactory, what was to take its place? The human mind, like nature, abhors a vacuum. What loyalty was to replace the loyalty to the national idea? The question compelled an answer. But as yet Iqbal had no definite answer. A number of lines of inquiry suggested themselves. They had to be explored. They *were* explored. There was, for instance, the cosmopolitanism of the Western intelligentsia. But it was a shallow doctrine, an elegant evasion of social responsibilities. Then there was the internationalism of the socialist movement with its belief in the brotherhood of man as the ultimate goal of human society. But socialism, in its pure and valid form, was inextricably linked with a materialist philosophy of history and a scientific dialectics which Iqbal found always impossible to accept. The reasons for this rejection were largely psychological, rooted in inhibitions and complexes derived from his childhood conditioning, and only indirectly intellectual.

There were to be a number of occasions in Iqbal's career when he had to choose between the certitudes of the past and the promise of the future. If one says that on such occasions he invariably chose the former it is not to suggest a derogatory judgment. It is merely to record a fact and record it honestly. Faced with the dilemmas created by his abjuration of the territorial nationalistic doctrine, he looked backwards—to Islamic history. For Islam in its most vital and fruitful phases had provided the basis for a loyalty which united human beings across the frontiers of land and sea, of race and colour. It had provided the basis for a loyalty which had superseded the tribal idea, first in Arabia where it had united a number of perennially warring tribes; it later unified the vast regions of the Near and Middle East into a single empire; and finally it extended the bonds of Islamic fraternity across Africa and Europe as far west as the Iberian Peninsula. To Iqbal the phenomenal growth of Muslim power from the eighth century onwards represented the movement and fulfilment of a spiritual idea, not a movement actuated and determined by certain temporal, economic and political urgencies. He saw in the rise and consolidation of the Caliphate a confirmation of the correctness of Islamic ideals—ideals based on an all-embracing system of polity which affirmed the oneness of God and the unity of all the faithful, independent of considerations of race and colour and accidents of birth. He quoted with proud approval the well-known remark of the famous Arab conqueror, Tarik, who, when he led his forces from Africa across to the coast of Andalusia, asked his soldiers to burn the boats in which they had crossed and cheered his home-sick followers with the declaration: 'Every country is our country because it is the country of our God.'

Here then was a foundation for a larger spiritual loyalty worthy of man and his destiny. Iqbal could accept it without equivocation or doubts. He would awaken the world of Islam, and in particular the Muslims of India, from the torpor of a despondent fatalism and stir them to activity in the name of the heritage of dynamic ideals which were that of Islam. He would lead them towards a new promised land of the spirit through the realization of the potentialities that lay dormant in their faith. This is how he puts it:

> In the darkness of the night,
> I will lead my weary caravan.
> My sighs will emit sparks
> and my breath will raise flames.

However, all this was still a complex of vague exultations and promptings of the heart. It had not yet acquired the sharp outline of a clearly seen and lucid perspective. The decision and the determination necessary to execute the decision, had yet to come; and even when it came it was not to be quite the thing he had hoped for or anticipated.

Meanwhile his stay in Europe was coming to an end. While still at Cambridge he had also studied for the Bar. This was a common practice among the Indian students who came to England for higher studies. For the legal profession was not as yet so overcrowded as it has become in recent years. It still provided an easy road, not only to social distinction, but also material prosperity; even at the worst it entitled one to an additional degree without any strain on one's intellectual resources and without much mental effort. Iqbal was called to the Bar in 1908. The same year he returned to India.

## CHAPTER IV

## In Search of Faith

Iqbal was thirty-five when he returned to India. Thirty-five is a critical age for man; the ancients, with some justification, regarded it as the half-way point of man's earthly journey. It is the time of life when most people feel the necessity of evaluating what has gone before, of reckoning up the loss and gain of experience, and of making decisions as to the future path from among a number of tantalizing possibilities. And this decision has to be made with the full knowledge that whatever the path of one's choice there is still at the end the same abyss beyond which no man can see. At twenty-five it is all different; the range of choice is seemingly infinite; deviations and digressions from the straight and narrow path of rectitude have about them the excitement of adventure. There is time to make mistakes and time to correct them. Not so at thirty-five, when each step that is taken appears irretrievable and errors of choice have an element of finality. And more. Thirty-five is the age at which, according to the mystical tradition, conversions occur and illuminations are vouchsafed to those who are seeking them. Dante, it may be recalled, was thirty-five when he lost himself in 'a wood dark and sombre' from which he was to be led by the guiding spirit of Virgil and furnished a vision of heaven and hell and the intermediate regions.

There is no evidence that Iqbal at thirty-five was blessed with any similar vision of terror and beauty, or that he went through a comparable crisis of the spirit. Perhaps such a crisis was not even possible in the peculiar ethos of India and in the world in which Iqbal lived and moved. The feudal economy had, it is true, broken down, but not yet the feudal values. Their rigid formalism still persisted in the society of which Iqbal was a part. It had its advantages and disadvantages. If, on the one hand, it prevented the Indian middle class from fully participating in the main current of modern history, it also provided an effective safeguard against the shock of any too violently disturbing an experience, on the other. For it provided a whole series of traditional, almost automatic constraints and consolations which had the anaesthetic effect of softening the immediacy and violence of the impact of experience upon the individual awareness. The individual, in fact, was never quite thrown entirely on his own resources as he had been increasingly in Europe ever since the Renaissance.

Nevertheless, it would be untrue to suggest that Iqbal at this stage in his life was at peace with the world. We have pointed out how his stay in Europe had brought him face to face with new problems, how it had started the process of reorientation. The result, despite all that Iqbal acquired in the way of knowledge, was actually more negative than positive: he had shed much that he had been inclined to take for granted in his early writings, but had not yet found anything to replace those beliefs. He had some intimation of the direction in which he was moving, but the ultimate goal lay as yet in the dim distance and its shape was not clearly visible. He was still seeking a faith and a philosophy of life; and in the next few years this quest was to become still more earnest and intense.

First, however, there were certain practical problems to be resolved. He had to take up the thread of his life where he had left it when he went to Europe. This fortunately did not present any great difficulty. There were the usual receptions and welcome which it was customary in India for the prodigals returning from abroad to receive; Iqbal had more than his share, for he had a very large circle of friends and admirers, and there is no reason to doubt that quite a number of fatted calves, real and not merely metaphorical ones, were killed in his honour. After these feasts, festivities and visitations were over, Iqbal settled down in Lahore to resume his teaching post at the Government College. He had gone to Europe only on study leave and his post had been kept open for him. What is more, his visit to Europe for higher academic attainments had proved to be a good investment: it had increased not only his prestige, but value in terms of salary for the Education Department. Most of his biographers record with pride that on his return his salary was raised to Rs 500 per month. The pride is understandable: in the days before the First World War few Indians were appointed to the higher grades of the Education Service, or indeed any other administrative service. A salary of Rs 500 per month, moreover, according to the actuarial standards then prevalent in India meant veritable riches. Iqbal had every reason to congratulate himself. The more so because, as a special concession, the authorities allowed him to combine his work as a Professor with legal practice, if he so desired. This concession was more or less a matter of formality. Iqbal had a profound interest in the history of Jurisprudence; towards the end of his life he intended, in fact, to write an authoritative treatise on Muslim Jurisprudence for which he had collected much material; but this interest did not extend to the actual practice of Law. He had little use for the futile intricacies, deceptions and dissimulations of the legal profession—particularly in the peculiar conditions of India where legal reputations have often been built on people's capacity for infinite quibbling. He never took his practice seriously and actually tried to avoid taking any more cases than were necessary to keep him financially solvent. As a result, he never made a name for himself at the Bar nor even cared to do so.

As a teacher he was stimulating, sympathetic and successful. Those who studied under him during the few years that he was at the Government College have borne witness to his great qualities in this direction: he was brilliant without being overwhelming, always took personal interest in his pupils and understood better than most pedagogues that the real function of a teacher, to quote Tagore, 'is not to explain meanings, but knock at the door of the mind'. Had he continued as a Professor there is no doubt that he would have achieved eminence in that line. But his heart was really not in the job; other yearnings and aspirations possessed him. He did not stay at the Government college for long. After about two years and half as a Professor he resigned his post in the Educational Service. The Principal of the college tried to dissuade him from this decision, but his mind was made up. The resignation from what appeared to be a lucrative post with excellent prospects for the future surprised many of his relatives and friends, and they naturally asked him what had impelled him to take this step. His answer was that he felt he 'could not freely express his ideas while in Government employment'.

This affirmation of his independence was important and symptomatic of that change in his personality which had been accelerated by his European experience. Indirectly, it was also linked with the crisis through which the Muslim community as a whole was passing at the time. It was a complex crisis and its manifestations and consequences were often contradictory and bewildering. On the one hand it was to create the tradition of Muslim 'loyalism' to the British, a tradition which accurately reflected the political conceptions of the founder of the Aligarh Movement; on the other, it was also to give rise to a vigorous movement of protest against the ruling power, represented by men like Moulana Abul Kalam Azad and Mohammed Ali who were later to play a decisive role in the Indian independence struggle.

To get some measure of this crisis it is necessary to have an idea of the historical background in which it originated. Somewhere in the first decade of the present century, an artificial but morbidly acute dichotomy was created in India's political life. Signs of this development had begun to be noticeable during the nineties of the last century, but it was in the first decade of the twentieth century that it became a continuous and permanent feature of Indian polity. The Aligarh spirit may have had points of conflict with the idea of all-India nationalism, but it is only after the beginning of the new century that this conflict acquired an active character.

A number of events helped to accentuate this process of alienation. There was Lord Curzon's brilliant idea of partitioning Bengal. This move was resented by the Hindus, and particularly the Hindu middle class which saw in it a threat to its economic domination of the life of the province. To the Muslims, however, it appeared to be a move favourable to their interests since it would increase their influence in the newly created province of Bengal, with Dacca as its capital. The opposition to this British move, which was almost wholly Hindu and very violent, resulted in the eventual annulment of the Partition. It was represented at the time and still continues to be represented as a victory for Indian nationalism. It proved to be in the long run a pyrrhic victory. It accentuated Hindu-Muslim tension, not only in Bengal, but all over India and it is no exaggeration to suggest that it damaged the relations between the two communities permanently. More important still, it convinced a considerable section of the Muslim bourgeoisie that it had more to gain by being faithful to the North Sea islanders who were ruling India than by co-operating with the Indian national movement whose dominant leadership, for all its protestations of patriotism, was swayed essentially by communal interests and impulses.

This conviction found practical expression in the foundation of the All-India Muslim League which Lord Minto, then the Satrap in India, who 'liked Indian Mohemmadans', regarded as a development of capital significance. This, it is worth noting, happened after the Partition of Bengal in 1905. It led later, in 1909, to influential Muslims demanding separate electorate and representation in the Morley–Minto Reforms. It was the first act of a drama which was to have its tragic denouement in August 1947.

But there was also another trend among the Indian Muslims. If events in India were alienating the Muslims from the Hindus, events in the world at large were alienating them from the British. The disintegration of the Ottoman Empire, which for the Indian Muslims in their highly emotional mood symbolized Islamic power, had begun; and this process was certainly accelerated, if not started, by British policy in the Near and Middle East and in the Balkans. Edward Thompson and G. T. Garratt in their *Rise and Fulfilment of British Rule in India* have succinctly summed up the situation:

> British foreign policy during these pre-War years added to Muslim discontent. One Mohammedan country after another was being absorbed by European Powers and the British were either privy to the arrangement, as in Morocco and Persia, or made no protest, as in Tripoli. The Balkan Wars of 1912–13 were considered part of a general attack upon Islam. Meanwhile the younger Indian Mohammedans were increasingly affected by the racial nationalism of the educated classes, and their co-religionists in other countries. Money was collected for a Turkish Red Crescent fund, while a common enmity brought a few Muslims into the extremist movement, which had lost most of its old Hindu bias.

To this trend belonged a group of brilliant young Muslim intellectuals like Dr Ansari, Moulana Azad, Moulana Shibli, and the Ali Brothers. Their writings and especially the periodical founded by Moulana Azad, *Al Hilal*, expressed the aspirations and moods of the more militant and catholic elements of the Muslim intelligentsia.

Where did Iqbal stand in relation to these events and developments? How did the political crisis in the world of Islam affect him? That he was deeply affected by it there is no doubt. It was completely to change the texture and content of his poetry.

But his reactions were not of an obvious and superficial nature. He witnessed the humiliations and defeats of the Islamic nations, and of the Muslims in India, with profound emotion, but at this stage did not join any active movement of protest. This was not because he was a loyalist, like many other eminent Muslims in India: he was, in fact, constitutionally incapable of ever being a loyalist and temperamentally was much more akin to the militant Muslim political leaders. But he was never himself a politician: the insincerities and compromises of the world of *realpolitik* always repelled him. So he preferred to remain outside any political activity and confined himself to his function as a poet and interpreter of the impulses which were stirring in the minds and hearts of his co-religionists.

Thus it was in the sphere of ideas that the crisis of Islam found an echo and articulation in his work. It developed in him that anti-modern and anti-Western bias which was to become increasingly pronounced as he grew older. For he equated modern civilization, which in effect meant Western civilization, with those acquisitive, aggressive and mercenary trends which revolted him. Simultaneously with the growth of this bias in his mind, another more positive trend began to manifest itself in his writings. He had always been attracted by the idea of Pan-Islamism, or the political as well as spiritual unity of all the Muslim nations of the world. This idea had been given currency by a remarkable Muslim preacher from Afghanistan, Saiyed Jamal-ud-Din Afghani, who travelled far and wide in the Near and Middle East during the nineteenth century and whose speeches in Turkey, Iran, Egypt and other Muslim countries had created a very great impression among the intelligentsia of those countries. Afghani's conception of a commonwealth of Islam, transcending territorial and national boundaries, confirmed certain ideas which had been germinating in Iqbal's own mind during his stay in Europe and they now took a more definite shape. He would preach the message of unity to the people of the Book, a message based not on the narrow nationalistic doctrine of tribal exclusiveness, but a broad, world-wide identity of spiritual purpose. Such a unity had, moreover, become an imperative and practical necessity in the face of the growing threat by Western imperialist powers to the very focus and centre of Islamic power—the Caliphate.

Hitherto in his verse he had largely been preoccupied with

amiable descriptive and lyrical themes; he had also written of India, her greatness and the need for Indian freedom and unity. But now the point of emphasis began to shift to purely Islamic motifs. First, there was the mood of frustration and disconsolate despair which possessed the Muslims of India at this time. He reflected it in his poetry, reflected it with an exquisite and ardent passion that was to move hundreds of thousands of people to the innermost depths of their souls. It was at this time that he wrote his famous 'Complaint' which became one of his most popular poems among his Muslim readers.

The 'Complaint' was written soon after Italy had grabbed Tripoli from the Turks. The event was only yet another incident in the process of progressive disintegration of the Ottoman hegemony over parts of Asia, Africa, and south-eastern Europe, but its repercussions among Indian Muslims, already harbouring a sense of grievance, were very far-reaching. Iqbal wrote his poem obviously under the stress of the emotions aroused by the fall of Tripoli. His poem is a kind of modern version of Job; only Job complained of his personal misfortunes to God, while Iqbal's 'Complaint' is communal and sets out to voice the grievances of his people against their God. It does so magnificently. The poet himself is the protagonist. He pleads with God for justice for the Muslims. Why is it, he asks God in effect, that while the ungodly and the unrighteous are allowed to prosper and flourish, the Muslims, who fear God and eschew evil and keep His commandments, languish in perpetual misery and are deserted by their God?

> There are other nations besides us;
> There are sinners amongst them,
> Humble people and others swollen with pride,
> Slothful, careless or clever.
> Many there are who are weary of your Name.
> But you bestow grace on their habitations,
> and your thunderbolts strike only our dwellings.

And getting even more vehement, almost angry with God, he goes on to say:

> The idols in the temple say: 'Muslims are gone.'
> And they rejoice that the guardians of *Ka'ba* are no
> more.

> They say: 'The world's stage in cleared of the
>                                                camel-drivers;
> they have fled with their Qu'ran in their armpits.'
> The worshippers of many gods laugh at us.
> Have you no feeling?
> Have you no regard for your Unity?

Iqbal read the 'Complaint', or rather chanted it as was his habit in a soft and melodious voice, at the annual meeting Anjuman-i-Himayat-i-Islam. The effect on his audience was tremendous. And not surprisingly. His earlier poem, the 'Cry of the Orphan', had expressed the mood of the Muslims in terms of a symbol. But now the total emotional reality was there for them to feel and appreciate in their being. They themselves were the Orphans—Orphans deprived not merely of the care and protection of their earthly parents, but abandoned by their very God. The anguish of self-pity filled them to the overflowing. There was sighing and sobbing and copious tears all round.

It was about the same time that he wrote another poem, shorter than the 'Complaint', but expressing the same sentiments of discontent and dissatisfaction and voicing the Muslim protest against the general order of things. The poet finds the time 'out of joint', like the Prince of Denmark. He is weary and sick at heart, and decides to leave the world. The angels take him to Heaven and he is ushered into the presence of the Prophet. The Prophet asks him:

> You who have come from the garden of existence
>                                  in the likeness of a fragrance
> What gift have you brought to present to us?

And the poet replies:

> Lord, I have found no tranquillity in the world
> Nor have I found the way of life for which I have
>                                                            yearned.
> There are thousands of flowers in the garden of
>                                                         existence,
> But I have not found one which possesses the
>                                            fragrance of loyalty.
> Yet I have brought for presentation one crystal,

> It contains something which even in paradise is not to
> be found.
> For the honour of your kindred is reflected in it:
> It contains the blood of the martyrs of Tripoli.

Iqbal recited this poem after the prayer at the King's mosque in Lahore before a vast congregation. Its effect on the audience was no less than that of the 'Complaint': if anything they were even more deeply stirred by the topical reference to the tragedy of Tripoli. Iqbal had so far been regarded as a poet of promise. He had his admirers among the intelligentsia; and the older poets like Hali and Dagh smiled approbation at him. He was also known outside the intellectual circles because of his association with the Anjuman-i-Himayat-i-Islam. But after his 'Complaint' and the poem on the martyrs of Tripoli he acquired an all-India reputation. The whole of the Muslim community looked to him for the interpretation of their deepest thoughts and feelings. He had a vast public among those Muslims who could read. And not only among those who could read. For poetry in India was still broadcast at least as much by word of mouth as by the printed word. And Iqbal's poetry was recited not only in the company of the select few, but at the street corners and coffee stalls and sung by vendors of betel-leaf. It had stirred in its poignant melody some sensitive chord of the Muslim heart.

Popularity, reputation, intellectual eminence Iqbal had now attained. He could have been successful even in the purely material sense of the term, but he never cared for success at that level. A lesser person than him might have been inclined to rest on his laurels; worse still, to lapse into smug self-satisfaction under the admiring and adulatory gaze of a by no means critical public. But Iqbal was always too honest with himself to fall a victim to complacency. He knew he had gifts of eloquence adequate to the purpose which he had set himself; he knew that he had a voice, more vibrant and moving than any of his contemporaries possessed; he knew he could become the authentic poet of an Islamic Renaissance which would extend far beyond the boundaries of India.

He knew all this, but he also knew that great poetry is not of the stuff of passing enthusiasms and exultations. The function of a poet is not only to interpret, but to create while interpreting. The poet has to have a vision of which he can be certain and which he can claim as his own. For where there is no vision poetry perishes. There were many other voices in India. They were quite content to sing in borrowed strains. Iqbal in his youthful years had been inclined to do the same. He had, often unconsciously, sometimes consciously, thought other men's thoughts and presented other men's flowers. But he knew that he could not live, as he was to put it later, 'with the breath of others'. He must, therefore, purge his poetry, purge his own being in other words, of all that was second-hand and alien. He must create in himself that hard and adamant core of faith, that framework of certitude and belief, which alone can transmute the ephemeral melody into the gold of inspired utterance.

It was not an easy task, this task of self-purification. It meant, first of all, getting rid of all his earlier enthusiasms. There was the sentimental heritage of the Western Romantics. That was easy to abjure, for it had only been the attraction of glittering surfaces. Then there was the enthusiasm for Sufi mystics and poets, for the song of pure delight of Hafiz in particular. It was difficult to outgrow this passion. In unguarded moments one reverted to it. One way of repudiating this influence was to denounce it publicly. Iqbal did so, did so with a violence that was to surprise everyone and shock many. The violence was in part a violence against himself: for it was really repudiating a part of himself, the old self from which he was struggling to break free. The yearnings to which he had referred in his letter to a friend were still yearnings and not a realization. The faith which he was seeking still evaded him, though the moment of illumination was drawing near.

CHAPTER V

## The Time of Unveiling

Meanwhile world events were fast moving to their climax of disaster. In 1907 Iqbal in his 'Warning to the West' had already cautioned the peoples of the West that their civilization was preparing to commit suicide and that a 'nest built upon a fragile bough cannot endure'. Nobody had heeded his warning; hardly anybody had read it. But his prophecy was now being fulfilled to its last bitter syllable. The 'nest built upon a fragile bough' had crashed. And what a crash it was! Some of the most advanced nations of the West, claiming to be the custodians of culture and civilization, had decided to revert to the morality of the beasts of prey and fallen on each other with a savagery unequalled in the history of mankind. The belligerents were trampling under foot all the civilized values from the Sermon on the Mount downwards; it was indeed a mass suicide. More than that, the warring nations were dragging the rest of the world with them into the abyss of war and senseless destruction.

Iqbal could have drawn some perverse pleasure from the fulfilment of his prophecy of woe. There is no reason to believe that he did, in fact, take any credit for having foretold the catastrophe. But, on the other hand, there is nothing to indicate that he was particularly moved by the European tragedy or felt it as a disaster that implicated him in any way. He had dissociated himself from the fate of the West. Perhaps, he had in some measure, though not wholly, dissociated himself from the fate of India as a national and territorial entity. He was primarily interested now in the destiny of Islam in the modern world; and the world crisis became real to him only in so far as it also affected the Islamic nations. The First World War was, of course, a threat to the Muslim nations; but it was also an opportunity for them to vindicate their faith, to disentangle themselves from the toils of Western diplomacy and strike out on a new path of their own. He would try to indicate this new path to them, to define their new goal.

However, as yet even the prospect of being the torch-bearer on this new path for the Muslims of the world, important and urgent though it was, seemed to take a secondary place on his list of priorities. He had been for the past seven years or more engaged on a personal quest of his own. In the same poem in which he had warned the West of the dangers that loomed ahead, he had also embodied a premonition, somewhat premature it is true but nevertheless significant, of the discovery that he was about to make. That poem, indeed, had begun with the intimation of the imminence of his discovery:

> The time of unveiling has come
> The beloved will reveal himself to everyone.
> The secret which has so long been veiled in silence,
> Shall now be revealed.
>
> Gone is the age of cup-bearers drinking in secret,
> The whole world shall become a tavern,
> And all shall drink.
>
> The ecstatics who have wandered so long
> Shall return to dwell in the cities;
> Bare-footed as ever they shall be,
> But they will partake of a new ecstacy.
>
> For the silence of Mecca has proclaimed to the ears
>                                         of expectancy;
> That the covenant which was made with
>                                         desert-dwellers,
> Shall once more be renewed.
>
> The lion which came from the wilderness
> And upset the Empire of Rome,
> I have heard angels declare
> That he shall awaken once more.

Iqbal was still involved in the old symbolism. The tavern and the cup-bearer are still there to remind us of his debt to the Sufi mystics. The labels and the bottles are the same, but there is a hint of change in the quality of the wine. The familiar language is there, but the terms of reference have changed and the terms themselves are struggling towards new significations. The wine is no longer meant purely for intoxication and self-forgetfulness as in the old days; it is to be a stimulus to activity—even to illumination. It is no longer the images of quiet innocence to which we are treated; we are told of the 'lion of the wilderness' once more ready to spring up from his sleep of ages. The contemplative ideal is about to be replaced by a doctrine of activism.

At the time when this poem was written, it is true, it represented a wishful projection into the future. But the wish was now on the point of being fulfilled. The time of unveiling had, indeed, come.

Outwardly, again, there is very little to indicate that anything so important was about to happen or that Iqbal had reached a crucial turning point in his career. On the contrary, uneventfulness was still the keynote of his life. His normal routine was as calm, as unperturbed, as ordinary as ever. He was living the life of a well-respected and sedate citizen of Lahore. He observed most of the proprieties and possibly a little more than the average pieties of his class and his community. He lived simply, almost frugally, without any spectacular exhibitions of largesse. At the same time his house was open to all his friends and even to strangers. They came, they partook of his meals—one of the favourite and most frequent dishes was apparently curry made from turnips—and of the far more delicious food for the mind provided by his brilliant conversation, which ranged over a wide field, anything, in fact, from the nature of the Godhead to the latest joke about local politicians; and they went away when they liked. There was no sense of formality, no elaborate ceremonies of entrance and exit such as surround great men; there was only an ambient and infectious atmosphere of friendliness. Equally, and it is worth recording, there was no touch of that Bohemian disarray or excessive heartiness which is sometimes associated with poets and artists. Iqbal had no use for exhibitionism in any shape or form.

Since he had resigned his post at the Government College, in what many of his friends thought a fit of impractical impetuousness, he had inevitably to devote more attention to his legal profession. But he saw to it that he restricted his commitments in this direction to the minimum. Those who knew him intimately have related how at the beginning of every month he made a rough estimate of what he would need for his living, and made it a point not to accept any more briefs than would cover his monthly expenses. Incidentally, till almost the end of his life it was a habit with him to keep a very careful account of his income and his expenses; and his domestic book-keeping would have conformed to the standards set by the most bourgeois of householders. This was undoubtedly a necessary detail, considering that Iqbal was never to earn more than a very moderate income. But it is an interesting, because surprising, trait in one whose philosophy repudiated all mercenary values and considerations of loss and gain. It underlines the contradictory and complex elements in his personality which he had himself acknowledged in his verse by saying:

> Iqbal himself is not aware of Iqbal,
> And this is not a joke, by God, this is not a joke.

This life of commonplace activity and preoccupations, however, was a mask, a screen behind which the spirit could exercise its delirious freedoms, could embark on its audacious adventures, without being observed by the restraining curiosity of what Kierkegard called the not-self, the objective world. On the surface there was a transparent ordinariness and calm. But underneath this deceptive surface was turmoil, perhaps even chaos—the kind of chaos which, as Nietzsche had observed (and Iqbal always had an affinity with Nietzsche, though he philosophically repudiated him), one needs to give birth to a dancing star.

The flow of poetry was continuing uninterrupted during these years. Much of the verse that at this time saw the light of the print was still in Urdu, but in private Iqbal was concentrating increasingly on experimenting with the Persian medium, though this was known only to his intimate circle and his wider public still knew him through his Urdu poetry. Then what had been hitherto more or less private news was made public.

The occasion for this announcement was provided by the annual meeting of the Anjuman-i-Himayat-i-Islam in Lahore in 1914. It had become an accepted tradition of this organization that Iqbal celebrated the annual session of the Anjuman by reciting a new poem on some appropriate Islamic theme: that was his special contribution to the cause of Islam. His poems were invariably successful in creating the right atmosphere of emotional fervour which had the effect of loosening the purse-strings and bringing contributions for the work of the Anjuman. At the 1914 annual session of the society, however, Iqbal did not recite a complete poem: he read out instead parts of a long poem in progress on an obtuse, philosophic theme. What is more, it was not in Urdu, but in Persian. And few among his audience could understand Persian, though doubtless many could read it with a certain degree of facility.

There was some disappointment among his listeners. It was not the Iqbal they had known and appreciated—lyrical, emotional and always capable of stirring the lachrymal glands to the point of exquisite excruciation. The ardent accents were no more: there was in its place deep reflection and the translucency of difficult and intricate thought. This was not what they had anticipated; this was not what they wanted and were prepared to pay for. There was general consternation. Puzzled eyebrows were raised: among the few who understood, there was a sense of apprehension. What was Iqbal trying to do and where was he heading?

These questions did not find an immediate answer. The poem was still unfinished. And it was not finished till some time later; and was actually published a year and half after the meeting at which parts of it were first read. Then there could be no doubt of the enormity of which Iqbal had been culpable and the storm broke over his head. Criticism was violent and copious, not at all stinted. Those who had admired Iqbal as a lyricist, as an interpreter of their own sentimental moods, as a virtuoso of amiable melodies now turned on him, with a fury inseparable from disappointed hopes and loves. It was not surprising. Iqbal in his poem had given no quarter to those whom he attacked; he could, by the rules of war, hardly expect any clemency of judgement. He had even committed the unforgivable sacrilege of attacking Hafiz of Shiraz in no uncertain or ambiguous terms.

But let us not anticipate. The literary and philosophic controversy which was started by the publication of the poem—entitled *Asrar-i-Khudi*, or 'Secrets of Self'—and which continues in interested circles to this day can only be understood by a slow and gradual process of disentangling its various essential threads from the unessential loose ends of emotion and knots of partisanship engendered by the work. We shall, therefore, proceed step by step.

The poem follows a formal pattern which has nothing startling, revolutionary or exceptional about it. It is written in the *Mathnawi* form, certainly one of the most respectable, if not the oldest, mode employed by Persian—and following them the Urdu poets. With its basic unit consisting of the rhyming couplet and an elastic structure, it has always been regarded as a more suitable medium for long and discursive poetical arguments than either the *Ghazal* or the *Rubai* (quatrain). It permits, moreover, of a wide range of variation of rhythm and cadence, of theme and motif, within the unity of framework provided by a general idea.

Iqbal in deciding to use the Mathnawi form had, above all, been influenced by the great Persian medieval poet and mystic Jalal-u-Din Rumi who founded the order of dervishes known as 'Maulawis'. There is little doubt that he took as his model Rumi's famous *Mathnawi-i-Ma'nawi*, or 'Spiritual Couplets', which has been described as the 'Qu'ran of Persia'. Of Rumi's long poem, the late Professor R. A. Nicholson, a friend and translator of Iqbal's *Asrar-i-Khudi*, has written in the *Legacy of Islam*:

> Its author professes, indeed, to expound the inmost sense of prophetic revelation; but any one looking through the work at random can see that its doctrines, interwoven with apologues, anecdotes, fables, legends, and traditions, range over the whole domain of medieval religious life and thought. Whereas in his odes he often writes from the standpoint of the mystic who sees nothing but God, the *Mathnawi* shows him as an eloquent and enthusiastic teacher explaining the way to God for the benefit of those who have entered upon it...

Professor Nicholson's remarks describe with surprising accuracy the scope and purpose of Iqbal's *Asrar*. The choice of Rumi's *Mathnawi* as his model was, therefore, no mere accident. Iqbal was guided in this choice by an inner necessity and a sense of identity of spiritual purpose with Rumi. He, too, saw as his main mission in life the exposition of 'the inmost sense of the prophetic revelation'. This may seem a redundant and superfluous mission, since the Qu'ran is accessible to most of the literate faithful and can be bought for a modest sum. But that was not how Iqbal saw the problem. For him the accessibility of the Qu'ran was no guarantee that its inner core of meaning was being understood—even by the learned divines, perhaps least of all by the learned divines.

The problem, as it presented itself to him, was twofold. First, there had to be a destructive process of negation and purification. He had lived through that process in his own being. He had, so he felt, cleared his own mind of all the tempting irrelevancies of borrowed thought. This process had now to be repeated on an impersonal plane. The world of Islamic thought had to be purged of all that was impure, meretricious and alien. During the centuries that had followed, the hard and crystal core of the word of prophetic revelation had become overlaid with layer after layer of false and delusive metaphysics. These excrescences had to be removed and the densities of superfluous growth cleared away before the heart of the Qu'ranic truth could be revealed.

In practical terms, the task reduced itself to elimination from the body of Islamic thought of all traces of Greek thought. For between the ninth and thirteenth century AD the world of Islam came under the spell of Greek ideas and these profoundly modified the Islamic outlook in every sphere—politics, arts, sciences, theology and metaphysics. The movement began in the reign of the liberal and enlightened Abbasid Caliph Ma'mun-al Rashid (813-33), or Ma'mun the Great. He founded the famous Academy at Baghdad, had Greek literature translated into Arabic, and opened his Court to Greek scholars and scientists. It was under his patronage that the Nestorian physician Hunayn ibn Ishaq al-Ibadi (809-73) started his career as a translator—a remarkably industrious career, for in addition to many mathematical and scientific Greek works, he was to translate in whole or in parts Plato's *Republic, Laws* and *Timaeus* as well as Aristotle's *Categories, Physics,* and *Magna Moralia.*

To Iqbal it seemed that it was precisely at this point that Islamic philosophy had gone astray from the straight and narrow path defined by the Prophet. It was the Greek philosophic influences, and specifically the influence of Platonic thought, which had destroyed the health and vitality of Islam. These influences—Iqbal would have called them contaminating infections—had transformed Islam from a dynamic philosophy of life triumphant and abundant into a passive, meditative creed at its best, and at its worst, into a pessimistic and stultifying fatalism. Indirectly, they had been instrumental in bringing about the decline and fall of Islam as a temporal world power. If the world of Islam had to be revitalized, and if it had to regain on the spiritual plane its original purity as well as its political strength and unity, then the first thing was to reject Plato and Platonism in whatever guise it presented itself. Iqbal in his *Asrar*, rejected Plato. He described him, rather uncharitably, as the 'leader of the old herd of sheep'.

This might have been permissible. But Iqbal went further. For Iqbal was logical; and logically the repudiation of Greek thought, and especially Platonism, led to repudiation also of the whole heritage of Sufi poets and mystics. For Sufism was indebted for much of its doctrinal basis to Plato, on the one hand, and to Vedanta of the Hindus, on the other. Its stress on the ecstacy of meditation, its pantheism, its leaning towards passivity and quietism—these were in sharp contradiction with the philosophy of action embodied in the Qu'ran. The process of purification, if it were to be carried to its logical conclusion, would demand the throwing overboard of Sufi ideas and tendencies. This meant, above all, repudiation of Hafiz and his tradition. For Hafiz was the arch-priest of Sufism and, as Dr Nicholson has aptly put it in the introduction to his translation of Iqbal's *Asrar*, 'venerated as master-hierophant' in Sufi circles. Iqbal repudiated Hafiz. He did more. He wrote in terms of unmistakable derogation of the great Persian poet:

> Beware of Hafiz—the wine dealer, whose cup contains nothing but deadly poison. He, the leader of the drunkards, is a sheep and has learned to sing and bewitch people. Avoid his goblet of wine, for he has put poison in it.

This is, obviously, exaggerated language of emotional recoil rather than considered intellectual judgment. It was bound to give offence to the many votaries of Hafiz and it meant alienating a large number of his contemporaries—for there was hardly any Urdu poet who had not at one time or another derived inspiration from the Hafizian ecstasy. There were angry protests from all sides at what was regarded almost as an act of blasphemy. Iqbal, however, was in no mood to recant or be penitent. He stuck to his guns, though as a minor concession to his critics he omitted the offending lines from the second edition of his *Asrar-i-Khudi.* But there could be no doubt that he had burnt his boats, like Tarik, having landed on a strange, and far-off philosophic shore. Even his more friendly and discerning critics voiced their bewilderment at the shift in his philosophic position. Thus his teacher and friend, McTaggart wrote to him after having read the translation of his *Asrar* in English: 'I am writing to tell you with how much pleasure I have been reading your poems. Have you not changed your position very much? Surely in the days when we used to talk philosophy together you were much more of a pantheist and mystic.'

Yet the philosophic shore upon which he had landed was, after all, not so strange and not so far-off. He claimed that he had only gone back to the original Qu'ranic inspiration and experience. In terms of geography, he had left Persia and Greece and returned to the desert sublimity of Arabia. He makes this quite clear in his poem:

> You who have gathered roses from the garden of Persia
> And seen the birth of spring in India,
> Now taste something of the heat of the desert,
> Drink the old wine of the date,
> Lay your head for once on her hot breast,
> Yield your body a while to her scorching wind.

The *Asrar* is essentially the imaginative story of this philosophic return.

The journey back to the original homeland of the Islamic Word involved many arduous tasks. Polemics with the siren voices of Greece and Persia was only one aspect of these tasks—perhaps not the most important. What was far more important was to justify the deed. This meant the elaboration of a philosophy of life, a *Weltanschauung,* capable of taking the place of what he had repudiated and rejected. In the *Asrar* that is the positive objective he set out to achieve.

It is not possible to give more than a bare outline of the

salient features of the concepts which form the philosophic basis of the *Asrar*. The poetic arguments, the parables, the anecdotes and apologues which, like Rumi in his *Mathnawi*, Iqbal uses in order to convince—one might almost say convert—us cannot be reproduced and are, perhaps, incapable of being reproduced except in his own words. For our purpose it is enough to have a rough sketch of the central idea and Iqbal, anticipating this, has provided what may be described as the digest of his philosophic system in a letter to his friend and translator, Dr Nicholson.

Iqbal begins by stressing the human ego, or personality, as the basic value and, indeed, the condition of being. Other systems of thought, and especially Sufism, had emphasized the need for the negation of the ego, for its annihilation and renunciation, and for the absorption of the individual self in the universal. Iqbal takes a standpoint dramatically and diametrically opposed to this. Not only should man not renounce his ego; he should do everything possible to develop it, to bring it to perfection—'to build his clay into manhood' as he puts it. 'The moral and religious ideal of man,' he writes, 'is not self-negation but self-affirmation, and he attains to this ideal by becoming more and more individual, more and more unique. The Prophet said, "*Takhallaqubi-akhlaq Allah* (Create in yourselves the attributes of God)". Thus man becomes unique by becoming more and more like the most unique individual. What then is life? It is individual: its highest form, so far, is the Ego (*khudi*) in which the individual becomes a self-contained exclusive centre. Physically as well as spiritually man is a self-contained centre, but he is not yet a complete individual. The greater his distance from God, the less his individuality. He who comes nearest to God is the complete person. Not that he is finally absorbed in God. On the contrary, he absorbs God into himself.'

And this process of the perfection and development of the ego has to take place not outside time and space, or the disembodied universe of thought detached from life and matter, but through struggle and striving in the world of time and space. 'Life,' Iqbal goes on to say, 'is a forward assimilative movement. It removes all obstructions in its march by assimilating them. Its essence is the continual creation of desires and ideals, and for the purpose of its preservation and expansion it has invented or developed out of itself certain instruments, e.g. senses, intellect, etc., which help it to assimilate obstructions. The greatest obstacle in the way of life is matter, nature; yet nature is not evil, since it enables the inner powers of life to unfold themselves. The Ego attains to freedom by the removal of all obstructions in its way. It is partly free, partly determined; and reaches fuller freedom by approaching the individual who is most free—God. In one word, life is an endeavour for freedom.'

In his attitude to time, too, Iqbal took a position completely contradictory to the Platonic, Sufi and Vedantist views. The world of time is not to be regarded as a world of shadows signifying nothing, a play of illusion on the edge of a void as the Hindu mystagogues had preached. Time is real and time is important. Indeed, eternity acquires significance, according to Iqbal, because there is time. 'Knowing not the origin of time,' he accuses his opponents, 'they are ignorant of immortality.' For him life is of time and time is of life.

Since the development and perfection of the ego, or personality, is the ultimate objective of all living, the problem of morality, of ethics in the largest sense, reduces itself for Iqbal into judging things, ideas, acts from the standpoint of that objective. 'Thus the idea of personality,' he tells us, 'gives us a standard of value: it settles the problem of good and evil. That which fortifies personality is good, that which weakens it is bad. Art, religion, and ethics must be judged from the standpoint of personality. My criticism of Plato is directed against philosophical systems which hold up death rather than life as their ideal—systems which ignore the greatest obstruction to life, namely, matter, and teach us to run away from it instead of absorbing it.'

But how and by what means is the ego to be strengthened and perfected? Iqbal's answer is, through love, and love not merely in its passive but active sense of positive desire. Intellect has a place in Iqbal's philosophy. In one of his later poems he was even to go so far as to say:

> The intellect too is a form of love,
> It is not wholly alien to the taste of vision,
> But this weakling has not the audacity,
> Of that other (Love), the ecstatic.

But the position assigned to intellect is secondary. The Apollonian way is subsidiary to the Dionysian. Yet it is as well to point out that Iqbal's conception of 'love'— *Ishq* is the Persian term he uses— was very special. He explains:

> This word is used in a very wide sense and means the desire to assimilate, to absorb. Its highest form is the creation of values and ideals and the endeavour to realize them. Love individualizes the lover as well as the beloved. The effort to realize the most unique individuality individualizes the seeker and implies the individuality of the sought. As love fortifies the ego, asking (*Su'al*) weakens it. All that is achieved without personal effort comes under *Su'al*. The son of a rich man who inherits his father's wealth is an 'asker' (beggar); so is everyone who thinks the thoughts of others. Thus, in order to fortify the ego, we should cultivate love, *i.e.*, the power of assimilative action, and avoid all forms of 'asking', that is, inaction. The lesson of assimilative action is given by the life of the Prophet, at least to a Mohammedan.

Up to this point the philosophic structure is by no means very original or even distinctive. It is a structure made up of a variety of source-materials. There are echoes here of Bergson, Nietzsche, even Hegel. The originality consists merely in the manner in which the various strands have been put together to form a mosaic which, if not always intellectually coherent, is, like Nietzsche's *Thus Spake Zarathustra*, imaginatively arresting.

Iqbal, however, does not content himself with creating an emotionally satisfying philosophic pattern. He goes on somewhat abruptly and arbitrarily, to link his doctrine of Egohood with the Islamic ethics as propounded by the Qu'ran and not as interpreted by latter-day scholastics and commentators. He argues that only the Qu'ranic morality and ethics have provided the correct basis for the integration of personality in historical experience. Elaborating the general principles of Muslim ethics, he envisages the movement of the ego towards uniqueness in three definite stages. The first stage is that of 'obedience of Law'; the second that of 'self-control' which is the highest form of self-consciousness or Egohood; and the final that of 'Divine Viceregency'.

It is on this last stage that he lays the greatest emphasis and it moves him to an eloquent adoration of the quality of what

## The Time of Unveiling

he calls *Niyabat-i-Ilahi*—Divine Viceregency. 'The *Naib* is the Viceregent of God on earth,' he writes, 'He is the most complete Ego, the goal of humanity, the acme of life both in mind and body; in him the discords of our mental life become a harmony. The highest power is united in him with the highest knowledge. In his life, thought and action, instinct and reason, become one. He is the last fruit of the tree of humanity, and all the trials of a painful evolution are justified because he is to come at the end. He is the real ruler of mankind; his kingdom is the kingdom of God on earth. Out of the richness of his nature he lavishes the wealth of life on others, and brings them nearer to himself. The more we advance in evolution, the nearer and nearer we get to him. In approaching him we are raising ourselves in the scale of life. The development of humanity both in mind and body is a condition precedent to his birth. For the present he is a mere ideal; but the evolution of humanity is tending towards the production of an ideal race of more or less unique individuals who will become his fitting parents. Thus the Kingdom of God on earth means the democracy of more or less unique individuals, presided over by the most unique individual possible on this earth. Nietzsche had a glimpse of this ideal race, but his atheism and aristocratic prejudices marred his whole conception.'

This conception of the *Naib*, or the Divine Viceregent, who sums up in himself the whole movement of human evolution towards perfection and uniqueness, is obviously apocalyptic. It will always lend itself to a variety of interpretation; and it is perhaps right that it should. The faithful will take it at its face value. The psychologists will see in it a delusive fantasy of an over-compensated inferiority complex or an apotheosis of the father-figure which in Iqbal's mind emerges literally as the unsurpassed super-ego, and the ultimate standard of individuality. The politically progressive critics will interpret the principle of 'Divine Viceregency' formulated with such eloquence by Iqbal, as a doctrine which trembles dangerously on the verge of the retrograde *Fuhrer Prinzip*.

And all these judgments and interpretations would be valid within their proper spheres and on their specific levels. But it would be a mistake to look for something like a systematic philosophy, or even a carefully worked out system of polity and ethics, in *Asrar-i-Khudi*. What we have here is the record of an imaginative flight into the realm of ideas, an audacious trajectory of thought which crosses from one mental height to another without giving us an opportunity of exploring the intervening valleys and abysses. The process of flight itself is so satisfying, so breath-taking, that we are inclined to forget or overlook the dangers and hazards that lie at the root of these eminences of thought. This is the more so because the argument for the flight is presented in terms of poetry. There are dull and pedestrian passages in *Asrar* where the didactic impulse takes supremacy over the imaginative; and this tendency in Iqbal was unfortunately to become more and more pronounced as time went on. But there are still moments, many moments, of purest inspiration where the utterance and the image has the hard radiance of a flawless diamond.

Philosophically speaking, perhaps, the most significant idea in *Asrar* was Iqbal's affirmation of 'desire' as the ultimate urgency and compulsion underlying the forward movement of life: he describes it as 'a noose for hunting ideals, a binder of the book of deeds'. In a country where it had become an automatic convention to reject the world of desire, at least in principle, where for two thousand years or more moralists had preached renunciation even if they had practised something else, it needed not an inconsiderable courage to assert the supremacy of desire, to stress its transcendental importance in the scheme of reality, and go to the very limit of its apotheosis by saying:

> The secret of life is in the seeking,
> Its essence is hidden in desire.
> Keep desire kindled in your heart,
> Lest your dust becomes a tomb.
> Desire is the soul of this world of colour and scent,
> The nature of everything is faithful to desire.
> Desire sets the heart dancing in the breast,
> And by its glow the breast is bright as a mirror.
> It gives to the earth the power of growing,
> It is the *Khizr* (Guiding Angel) to the Moses of
>                                           perception.

This was salutary; it was refreshing; but it was also more. It succeeded at some strange and luminous point to capture the *Zeitgeist*, the spirit if not of the time, at any rate, of the *milieu* in which Iqbal lived and moved. It seems to be the paradox of all revivalistic movements that they partake of the progressive trends of history; they represent the forward amplitude of time in its involutionary phase; and the revivalists themselves, even when they recoil most violently against the present and the future, are reflecting some contemporary urgency but reflecting it in inversion. Iqbal was always aware of the present, even agonizingly aware, though he often tended to interpret the present in terms of the categories of the past. His philosophy of action, of creative dynamism, for all its harping back for sanctions to the Qu'ran and the Prophetic revelation, was essentially rooted in the necessity of modern times as it presented itself to the particular group to which he belonged.

This is often overlooked; but it is important not to overlook it, if we are rightly to relate Iqbal to his age. His ideas represented the continuation, perhaps the fulfilment, of the Aligarh Movement. Sir Saiyed Ahmed Khan, too, had preached the need for an activist view of life and the rejection of fatalism. But Sir Saiyed's thought was naive, his arguments at times rudimentary. In Iqbal the idea has acquired maturity and gravity; the message is articulated on an adult level of consciousness; but the idea and the message are the same. They corresponded with the needs of his community and his class. He was asking the Muslims, and primarily the Muslim middle-class intelligentsia, to develop their 'egos', to stand on their own feet, to get going, in fact. That was the way to create a destiny for the Muslims in India as elsewhere. In this correspondence lies the strength and weakness of his philosophy.

The implications of the philosophical basis of *Asrar* were realized by few even among the Muslims at the time when it was first published. It was admired by some and criticized by many more, but hardly anyone understood where its argument led. Yet in the next quarter of a century its meaning was to become crystal clear. Iqbal had anticipated the latent mood of his community by some twenty-five years. In one of his poems he was to claim:

> I am waiting for the votaries who arise at dawn,
> Happy they who shall worship my fire,
> I have no need of the ear of today,
> I am the voice of the poet of tomorrow.

In the larger sense this claim can hardly be justified. But if we take this in a restricted sense as being applicable to the development of a particular class and group, then the claim undoubtedly possesses substance. It cannot be denied that within the next few decades many votaries were to arise to worship his fire.

# CHAPTER VI

## Message of the East

With the publication of *Asrar-i-Khudi* begins the mature phase of Iqbal's poetry. The *Asrar* was followed two years later by the publication of *Ramuz-i-Bekhudi* (Mysteries of Selflessness). The *Ramuz* is in the same Mathnawi form and in Persian. It pursues the theme of the earlier poem on another level. The *Asrar* had dealt with the problem of individual personality in relation to the problem of its own internal integration and development. The second Mathnawi concerns itself with the relationship of the individual personality to the collective will and purpose, to society in fact. The essential idea is that the individual through identification with the group-consciousness fulfils himself.

> The individual when he loses himself in the group,
> Like the expansion-seeking drop, becomes the ocean.

The use of the term 'loses' is startling and ambiguous: for it runs contrary to the philosophy of the earlier poem where the whole world is shown as being 'lost' in the perfect and most developed personality. But it is possible that what Iqbal means is not so much the absorption of the individual will in the collective as the amplification of the former through identification with the latter. Iqbal accepts the gregarious pattern of life and subjects the various social philosophies, modern and ancient, to his particular tests. He takes Marx to task for building his socialism on the equality of stomachs rather than that of the spirit. Western conceptions of democracy are rejected because they have no place for unique individuals in them since they are based on 'counting heads rather than weighing them'. Other social philosophies and politics are found equally wanting. All except one—Islam. Only Islam, in its pristine purity, provided a social system through which the individual could realize his deepest potentialities. He had put this argument in prose for the benefit of posterity as early as 1916 in a note on Muslim democracy written in the *New Era*:

> The Democracy of Europe—overshadowed by Socialistic agitation and anarchical fear—originated mainly in the economic regeneration of European societies. Nietzsche, however, abhors the 'rule of the herd' and, hopeless of the plebian, he bases all higher culture on the cultivation and growth of an aristocracy of Supermen. But is the plebian so absolutely hopeless? The Democracy of Islam did not grow out of the extension of economic opportunity; it is a spiritual principle based on the assumption that every human being is a centre of latent power, the possibilities of which can be developed by cultivating a certain type of character. Out of the plebain material of life Islam has formed men of the noblest type of life and power...

This is audacious affirmation, a characteristic example of Iqbal's mode of reasoning by seductive emotional assertions. But it is hardly convincing either as an argument or as a statement possessing historical exactitude. Certainly, it did not convince any but the already convinced. The world of objective reality has its own logic and its own dynamics; the historical process is impervious to poetic fantasies, no matter how enchanting. And events in the world obstinately refused to correspond either to Iqbal's prognostications or his desires. The World War was drawing to its close. One of the indirect consequences of the defeat of the Central and Associated Powers was the end of the tenuous hegemony of the Ottoman Empire in the Near East, Africa and south-east Europe. The Caliphate had crumbled under the weight of its own inequities and corruption; the external pressure had only provided the *coup de grace*. Upon the ruins of the Holy Muslim Empire, which may have been Muslim but had long since lost any claims to holiness, were about to arise a number of national states—a development similar to, though much more confused than, the growth of national states in Europe on the ruins of Christendom in Europe several centuries earlier.

The reaction of the Indian Muslim intelligentsia to the break-up of the Caliphate, or Khilafat, was typical: it was emotional, unbalanced to the point of being hysterical. They had identified themselves with this last symbol of Islam's spiritual and temporal power and looked upon its destiny as their own. Its unhappy fate represented to them their own humiliation and defeat. The cup of their bitterness was now full almost to overflowing. In its extreme form the sense of grievance and defeat even manifested itself as a 'Back to Arabia' movement. But on its more intelligent levels, it expressed itself as a political movement directed against the British who had undoubtedly contributed something to the collapse of the Caliphate as a temporal power.

This had one positive result. Hitherto the Muslim leadership, if it had not been hostile to the Congress movement, had maintained a lukewarm and reserved attitude towards it. But common misfortunes brought the Muslim leadership on the same political platform as the predominantly Hindu Congress leadership. The Khilafat and the Home Rule issue became identified; the streams of Hindu and Muslim nationalism had achieved a momentary conjunction; and there were wild scenes of Hindu-Muslim fraternization. But the confluence was artificial. The unity was a marriage of convenience rather than of true minds; and it did not endure, partly because it was not allowed to, and partly because there was no real understanding of each other's problems on either side.

Iqbal himself took very little part in the political agitation that shook India after the First World War. He wrote a few satirical verses against those who still found it possible to collaborate with the Alien Power, but did nothing more. Many of his friends were drawn into the political movement, but he stood aloof. Yet, it would be wrong to suppose that this aloofness signified indifference or callousness either to the cause of the Khilafat or Indian freedom. The latter cause now only aroused in him a wistful melancholy, though it had stirred him in his younger days. But the Khilafat was a different matter. All his hopes and dreams of a theocratic Islamic Commonwealth, the Kingdom of God on earth, transcending the narrow national and territorial boundaries, and rising to a loyalty higher than that of race or colour, were bound up with that institution. However decadent and weak, it represented the principle of continuity in the Islamic fraternity; it was a link with a great and glorious past. The fact that it had vanished into thin air was heart-breaking and unbearable.

For a moment, however, the hope revived. The rising star of Kemal Ataturk heartened him. Perhaps, after all, his prophecy of Islamic revival was to be fulfilled through Kemal's efforts. He was always impressed and cheered by any distinctive individual achievement: it provided a practical verification of his philosophy of Egohood. But the star on the Anatolian horizon proved to be a false portent. As soon as he had attained power, Kemal, with his abundant energy and good sense, began to clear all the lingering cobwebs of theocratic obscurantism, disestablished the religious institutions, and set about creating a modern secular state in Turkey. This was the last straw and Iqbal's disillusionment was complete.

But he was not the man to give up his ideals easily. In fact, the more the movement of events proved them to be impractical and unrealizable the more desperately he clung to them—desperately like people cling to hopeless passions. Each disappointment and disillusionment made his heart grow fonder—of the unattainable. There is a couplet of Rumi:

> They said: it is not be found
> We have sought for it long and in vain.
> He said: that which is not to be found
> Is what I desire.

A more accurate description of Iqbal's own approach to ideals would be difficult to find.

The world was proving exasperatingly refractory to his wishes. But what of it? He still had his own world of absorbing subjectivity. He could retreat into himself as he was to put it in a verse which may well have been written about this time in his life though it appeared in a later collection:

> Since you do not find in this world
> The beloved who knows how to minister to the heart,
> Be lost in yourself and uphold
> The honour of love's ardent ways.

He followed his own advice. He retreated into himself. The world of fantastic fulfilments became a satisfying substitute for the world of reality which would not listen to his words of wisdom. His verse acquired the acid flavour of disappointed purpose. Like the angry

Biblical prophets, he took up denunciation as one of his main preoccupations. He judged and he condemned contemporaries and contemporary values. Capitalism, imperialism, democracy, socialism, technique, all came in for criticism. But most of all he condemned the doctrines of territorial nationalism, racialism, and the seductions of the false graces of Western civilization. For these were destroying the spiritual unity of Islam and were preventing the realization of the destiny which was that of Islam. His poetry had always set out to be a critique of life; under the stress of these various exasperations and disenchantments, it tended to become a perpetual pronouncement of anathemas. But even at its most exasperated and angry moments it still possessed a music that could move the soul. And that saved it from degenerating into arid didacticism.

But life was not all bitterness and disappointment. There were compensations; there were even triumphs, minor triumphs, but still triumphs. First, there was fame and recognition. He now occupied a position in the world of Urdu letters which was undisputed, although by now he was writing almost wholly in Persian. Delhi and Lucknow may have charged him with provincial lapses, but he was too big for any criticism to shake his reputation. There were other poets who could claim all the perfections in the world, where poetry was of the stuff of infallibility of form. Iqbal's verse, on the other hand, had faults, many grave ones, but it had an amplitude and compass which none other could come within streets of claiming.

His fame, moreover, had now spread beyond the frontiers of India and that, in a way, settled the matter. For Indian intelligentsia invariably measured its accomplishments by the yardstick of Western, and especially British, recognition. And Iqbal had been recognized in Britain. Professor R. A. Nicholson had translated his *Asrar-i-Khudi* under the title of *Secrets of Self*. The book was published by Macmillan in 1920 and it had attracted some attention in England. Discerning critics like Professor Browne, Herbert Read, E. M. Forster had spoken amiably of it and recognized in it a work possessing gravity and beauty. But it was too esoteric for the average reader to understand and the great body of English-reading public showed no interest in it. There never developed in England any Iqbal vogue comparable to the popularity which Tagore enjoyed for a time after the First World War.

And for several reasons. Iqbal's poetry was of a very different quality to that of Tagore's. Tagore's diffuse and humane mysticism fitted in well with the post-war mood of desolation: it provided a sedative and an anodyne. Iqbal's verse brought no such sense of comfort. It did not correspond to the popular conception of an Eastern poet as a singer of delectable futilities to which Fitzgerald's translation of Omar Khayam's *Rubiayat* had given widespread currency. Iqbal fitted into none of these categories. His poetry was abstruse, sounded harsh in tone, provocative and even querulous. It could have no wide popular appeal. There was also the difficulty of translation. Dr Nicholson's translation was adequate in the sense that it conveyed accurately Iqbal's argument. But poetry is not only argument, or even sense; it exists in a dimension which ultimately transcends both argument and sense. The task of translation of poetry is, therefore, always one of great difficulty, the more so where the translation involves languages so different in structure and association as Persian and English. Dr Nicholson did his best, but he could not and did not succeed in recreating the melody and music of the original, nor the wealth of associations of certain images and terms, much less the undertones of emotion. *Secrets of Self* never went into a second edition and is today almost unobtainable.[1]

But in India what mattered was that it had been published in England: that fact by itself entitled Iqbal to an unchallenged claim to eminence among his contemporaries. Furthermore, he was soon knighted by the Government 'in recognition of his pre-eminent contribution to literature'. The British in India had long ago discovered the weakness of the Indian middle class for British heraldic titles and honours; this gave them a wonderful opportunity of buying loyalty on the cheap. At first the higher titles, like knighthoods, were conferred mainly on outstanding loyalists in the political and bureaucratic fields. But towards the second decade of the twentieth century a more liberal policy, as a part of the general policy of reform, was applied in this sphere. The claims of the sciences and of literature began to be considered

1. That was the situation in 1949. Since then, of course, all of Iqbal's works have been published.

at the appropriate seasons for the distribution of honorific crumbs. Tagore had been knighted; Iqbal could be given no lesser title. One Hindu literary knight had to be balanced against a Muslim literary knight: that was impartial enough.[1]

The surprising thing, however, was not that Iqbal was given the title, but that he accepted it—and that in 1923. He had in the past made fun in his verse of those who sought titles and honours from the Government. He had attacked the Muslim deputation which had gone to London to plead with the British Government on the question of Khilafat. But now, when temptation came his way, he found it impossible to resist it. By that act he placed himself on the same level as the Indian intelligentsia of his time and generation. Only he made it a condition of his acceptance of the title that, simultaneously, the title of *Shams-ul-Ulema*—a special title created for the purpose of honouring achievements in Urdu literature—should be conferred on his old friend and teacher, Moulvi Mir Hassan. Iqbal was always loyal to his teachers, Mir Hassan and Arnold, even if his loyalty to his own ideals was in practice never quite so steadfast.

Knighthood or no knighthood, the business of writing poetry was there; and Iqbal was nothing if not prolific. In addition to his two major works *Asrar-i-Khudi* and *Ramuz-i-Bekhudi*, which were written during the war years, he was writing a great deal of minor and occasional verse, though none of it had yet been brought together in a collection. Soon after the War he wrote two longish poems, namely, *Talu-i-Islam* (The Dawn of Islam) and *Khizr-i-Rah* (The Guide of the Way). These embodied his reaction to the political turmoil around him and, in particular, to the crisis of the Muslim world following the collapse of the Caliphate. They break no new ground nor do they contain any ideas which Iqbal had not already expressed. They represent variations on the theme to which Iqbal was to return again and again with an ecstatic vehemence—the theme of Pan-Islamism, of Muslim unity across all national and racial frontiers. In these poems Iqbal once again warns his co-religionists to beware of the dangers of territorial patriotism and he especially

1. Tagore, of course, renounced his knighthood after the Jallianwala Bagh massacre in the spring of 1919.

asks the Indian Muslims not to be taken in by the snares of the constitutional reforms which had been introduced to appease the political discontent.

Both *Talu-i-Islam* and *Khizr-i-Rah*, despite the popularity which they naturally enjoy among Iqbal's Muslim readers, are essentially parochial in their inspiration. This cannot be said of his collection of Persian verse which appeared in 1923 and was called *Payam-i-Mashriq* (Message of the East). It is a work of some importance and, in parts, of great beauty. Though it possesses no formal unity of structure—it consists of four distinct parts—it has, nevertheless, a thematic coherence and emotional consistency. There are redundancies, repetitions, even irrelevancies as there are always in Iqbal's work. But there is depth of feeling and at times even grandeur of thought. And it sustains the interest magnificently.

The collection, as the title suggests, was intended to be an answer, or rather a return of gifts, to Goethe who had acknowledged his debt to the East in his *Ost Westerliche Diwan*. The book begins with an introduction written by Iqbal himself—a rare thing, indeed. But the introduction, alas! is the least satisfying part of the *Payam-i-Mashriq*. It discusses the influence of Eastern thought and poetry on German thought and literature, with special emphasis on what Goethe and other German poets owed to the Persian poets—to Nizami, Sadi, and Hafiz. The discussion of what has been described as the 'Eastern Movement in German Letters' is neither very profound nor very illuminating; it tells one little that one could not get from any reference book; it is descriptive and rather verbose. This is disappointing, for Iqbal in his prose as in his verse was rarely dull. Iqbal seems to have been aware of this defect in his introduction, for he regrets at the beginning that he has not been able to discuss the subject 'in some detail' as he had intended, because he could not obtain certain books and journals which he needed for the purpose.

The *Payam* is dedicated to Amir Aman Ullah Khan, then the king of Afghanistan. This is significant. It would appear that Iqbal at this time entertained high hopes of this youthful, progressive, but ill-fated monarch who had shown unmistakable signs of independence of spirit and, as a result, made himself very unpopular with the British, especially because he had repudiated their right to control Afghanistan's foreign policy in return for a subsidy paid, with customary generosity, from Indian revenue—an act which was the real cause of the third Afghan War. The dedicatory poem is in a somewhat archaic style. It offers Aman Ullah much useful advice as to how he should conduct himself in his kingship. Describing him as 'young in years but mature of purpose', Iqbal ends his admonitions thus:

> Raise the goblet of love and start it on its round,
> In your mountain kingdom renew the message of love.

Unfortunately, Iqbal was one of those poets who are fated to be disillusioned in all their living heroes. King Aman Ullah did, in fact, start the goblet of love on its round, and many other goblets besides. Inspired by the example of the Ataturk's magnificent efforts in Turkey and by a trip to Europe with his queen, which included a visit to the Soviet Union, he started to modernize the country systematically. For this act of courage he had to pay with his crown; the revolt organized by the Mullahs, the orthodox divines, and almost certainly subsidized by a foreign power, was successful in chasing him out of Afghanistan. By a strange irony, when Nadir Shah, who was to succeed Aman Ullah after a period of confusion and assassinations, passed through India on his way to Afghanistan, among the Muslim leaders who met him at the Lahore railway station was Iqbal. It has been recorded that, thinking that Nadir Shah might be in need of money, Iqbal offered him his meagre savings—an offer which was graciously refused. But all this belonged to the future. In 1923 Iqbal still had great expectations of Aman Ullah—expectations that the new monarch would transform his mountainous kingdom into a model Islamic state based on Iqbal's concepts of Muslim polity.

The first of the four sections into which the *Payam* is divided is entitled 'The Tulip of Sinai'. It consists of one hundred and sixty-three quatrains; and it represents the main body as well as the essential core of his 'message'. The choice of the title has an overt symbolic significance. In Indo-Persian poetry the tulip is intimately associated with love—profane no less than sacred; it is also indirectly associated with the ecstacy of forgetfulness. But forgetfulness in this case has a very special meaning; this fact is emphasized by the juxtaposition of the symbol of love, and the ecstatic oblivion associated with love, with another symbol—Mount Sinai. It was on Mount Sinai that Moses received his illumination, his vision of God. The ecstacy of forgetfulness is thus equated with the ecstacy of illumination, of vision. For the vision of God involves at once utter forgetfulness and the ultimate condition of awareness; forgetfulness of all that is inessential and awareness at the deepest levels of the being. So at least the mystics of every age, country, and clime—Vedantists, Sufis, Platonists, Christians—have maintained.

But there is the rub. For it was precisely this mysticism in its Sufi, Vedantic, Platonic and Christian variations which Iqbal had so unequivocally and irrevocably abjured in his *Secrets of Self*. In view of the passionate repudiation of the Sufi and Neo-Platonic experience and doctrine in the *Asrar*, it is bewildering to find that there is scarcely anything in the cycle of quatrains with which the *Payam* begins which could not be reconciled with, and even directly related to, mystical conceptions and their variants. Some, indeed, are soaked through and through in the Sufi wine, as for instance, the following:

> O Guardian of Ka'ba, perhaps you do not know
> That to the world of love everything is the ultimate
> judgement,
> For here there is no sin, no account of loss and gain,
> There is no Muslim and no Infidel.

True, there are also some quatrains in which Iqbal is anxious to stress the idea of Egohood; others in which he dwells on his concept of Islamic internationalism. For instance:

> We are not Afghans, We are not Turks or Tartars,
> We are of one Garden and of one branch.
> The thought of colour and smell is anathema to us,
> For we are nurtured by the same new Spring.

Or again, the quatrain which precedes the one just quoted, ends with the emphatic assertion:

> Is Arabia proud of colour, blood, arteries and skin?
> Then abjure Arabia, too.

But these quatrains, or others like them, do not form an

essential part of the main theme. They might even have been after-thoughts. For it is not beyond the bounds of possibility that most of 'The Tulip of Sinai' cycle was composed, at least in its initial draft, much earlier than the *Asrar*, and that it was later revised and added to in order to bring its argument into alignment with Iqbal's new philosophy of Egohood. On the other hand, it may well be that in these quatrains we witness a case of imaginative return to a point of view, or rather a mode of feeling, which Iqbal had so ostentatiously rejected. Such returns are not unknown; they are psychologically even inevitable. *On revient toujours au prémier amour*. And this applies to philosophic loves as well. Iqbal certainly did return and in one of his poems he was to acknowledge this fact ruefully:

> And there are times
> When the traveller remembers
> The stage he has left behind...

There is more than a momentary remembrance of things past in 'The Tulip of Sinai', more even than nostalgic longings acting as a powerful psychological compulsion. There is a sense of unresolved emotional and intellectual conflict. Yeats has remarked that 'one makes poetry out of one's quarrel with oneself'. In the first part of the *Payam* the intimation of Iqbal's quarrel with himself is unmistakable; and it is this quarrel, this inward conflict, which invests his verse with that quality of sustaining and sustained tension which is of the very essence of poetry.

Yeats' theory of the origin and source of poetry can be extended and amplified. One makes poetry not only out of one's quarrels with oneself, but also out of one's quarrels with the world. Poetry very often is a protest against the subjective and objective conflicts which are part of the condition of humanity, or alternatively, an attempt at reconciliation of these agonizing oppositions. If the first section of the *Payam* articulates that sense of internal conflict which Yeats regarded as the source of poetic inspiration, the rest of the book reflects something of Iqbal's quarrel with the world.

The second part of the *Payam* is called 'Thoughts'. It consists of a series of poems unrelated to any consistent thread of argument or emotion. Some are in the nature of incidental descriptive verse. Others deal with diverse philosophic themes such as the 'Dialogue between Love and Knowledge' and the 'Dialogue between God and Man'. There are also some exquisite lyrical poems, like the 'Music of the Stars'. There is an address to Kemal Ataturk, written in 1922. There are occasional satirical epigrams, like the one on 'Democracy' where Iqbal warns us to beware of the democratic idea because, as he puts it, 'from the brain of two hundred donkeys it is not possible to extract the thought of one man'.

The third section entitled 'The Remaining Wine' is made up of a series of ghazals, not all of equal merit. The last and final part—'The Image of the West'—begins with a long poem, which gives this section its title. It is the message which he wishes to convey and the message is, in fact, contained in the first four lines:

> O breeze take this message from me to the wise
> men of the West,
> That Intellect since it opened its wings has become
> more of a prisoner.
> For Love strikes the heart like lightning while
> Intellect only domesticates it.
> Love is more brave than Intellect, that practicer of
> deceits.

From this Iqbal goes on to offer his poetic *obiter dicta* on a variety of subjects from the League of Nations to Hegel, from the 'Worker's Cry' to the 'Evils of the West'. He passes judgment on the whole body of modern thought and literature. He judges everyone of importance—Hegel, Locke, Bergson, Lenin, Kant, Schopenhauer, Nietzsche, August Comte, Byron, Browning and Einstein. These judgments are from his own very individual point of view; and they are not always complimentary. Karl Marx is charged with being unaware of himself; and of Nietzsche he says that 'though his being was a believer, his intellect was an infidel'. In one poem Hegel is confronted with Jalal-u-Din Rumi; in another Rumi is confronted with Goethe. The idea is to weigh these representatives of Western thought and literature with the highest norm of man's spiritual attainment, symbolized in Iqbal's mind by Rumi. Needless to say that it is the Easterner who is shown as possessing the greater gravity. The Westerners are

# Message of the East

by implication found wanting.

All these random but provocative judgments are interesting. They illuminate Iqbal's own frame of values and as such are significant. They cannot be taken as possessing any objective validity; and those who attempt to do so only make themselves and Iqbal look ridiculous. Every poet has a right to be polemical. Iqbal exercised this right to the full. But it is in the very nature of polemics that they cannot claim enduring value. Their interest wanes with time. Iqbal's polemical verse is no exception to this rule: if anything, it is more than usually subject to the law of diminishing significance. It smells strongly of mortality.

But what of the 'Message'? Does that, too, smell of mortality? Appreciation of poetry is a very personal and private affair, determined by personal and private factors. Any answer to these questions, therefore, cannot help being a matter of private and personal opinion. But before we attempt to give that opinion let us examine the message itself. For what is that message and where is it to be found?

The answer is that it is to be found in the cycle of quatrains which comes at the beginning of the *Payam*. It is very brief and very long. It is very simple and very complex. It is brief because it can be summed up in one word—Love; it is very long because that word is only a symbol behind which is hidden a whole universe of experience, an infinitude of feeling and apprehension, which cannot be encompassed in any language known to man. It is very simple because it evokes in most people at some level or point a chord of identity of emotion; and it is very complex because once we begin to analyse the concept and start arguing about it there is no end to analysis and argument.

Iqbal was aware of all this; and he really does not try to argue about something which is ultimately beyond argument and, perhaps, beyond reason. He merely affirms. He affirms the supremacy of Love as the way to the ultimate revelation of truth. He affirms more than that: he affirms that Love itself is that ultimate revelation of truth, that the way itself is the end:

So intoxicated am I with the delight of the journey,

That there is no other destination before me
But the stones of the path.

Here, then, the process is equated with the culmination of the process. Love is apotheosized. And because Love is apotheosized, so the heart, which is regarded as the seat and centre of Love, is elevated to the status of the supreme guide of human destiny. Not the mind which is the source of Intellect—that practicer of deceits—but the heart is the mediator between man and God. 'Logic is from Satan, Love is from God,' so Rumi had said. Iqbal reiterates this judgment. He does more than reiterate Rumi's judgment: he amplifies it. The heart is not just the mediator: it is the thing itself. In an ecstatic utterance he says:

My heart, O my heart, my heart,
You are my ocean, my boat and my shore as well!

And this ecstatic and imaginative metaphysics leads us to a passionate invocation to Love:

Come, O Love, O mystery of our hearts,
Come, you who are all our strivings and all our
                                        achievements.
These creatures of dust have grown old,
Create a new Adam from this, our clay.

This is translation. It is not the thing itself; it is not even a pale shadow of the original. Moreover, the enduring and the ephemeral, the mortal and the immortal, are human concepts. They are, as such, bound up with the tormenting relativity of man's mind which is never more relative than when it is trying to cast off its bonds of relativity. Nevertheless, some at least of those who have read 'The Tulip of Sinai' in the original must always be haunted by the feeling—it would be exaggeration to say conviction—that there are lines in it which are of immortal stuff. That is as near we can get to an answer to our questions.

CHAPTER VII

# A Chapter of Deeds

In a biography chronology has a certain manifest importance and it is, therefore, pertinent to mention that in 1923, when the *Payam* appeared, Iqbal was already fifty. This is an age at which in India, at any rate, public men begin to qualify for their title to venerability; an age at which most people feel inclined to do some stock-taking of their past and prepare a balance sheet of their successes and failures. Iqbal had a great deal on the credit side. In the realm of poetry he had achieved much. This achievement was acknowledged by all even if few understood his poetry or philosophy. He virtually dominated the literary landscape in the Land of Five Rivers; and even outside the Punjab his eminence could not be challenged, even though the pharisees in Uttar Pradesh and Delhi showed a degree of ostentatious reserve in assessing the importance of his work. From a purely worldly point of view, he had not much to show in the shape of an impressive bank balance and title deeds to real estate, but at least he managed to maintain himself, despite his poetic vocation. He was respected widely for his intellectual gifts and was in every sense an intellectual giant among the mediocrities that surrounded him. All this represented no mean achievement.

There was, however, a debit side to the account; and for him that deficit had an importance. He had set himself the task of transforming the world of Islam, transforming it not only by providing it with a new intellectual impetus, a healthy leavening of new thought, but by direct action. For he had formulated a worldview which had not merely to be thought out and perfected in a mental ivory tower, but had actually to be lived and worked out in practice. His was essentially a philosophy of dynamism, of action; a philosophy which he claimed was founded on the hard rock of Qu'ranic Revelation. And of the Qu'ran he was himself to say that it is a book which emphasizes 'deed rather than idea'. There were ideas enough in his life, but where were the deeds which were to transform and inspire Muslims, not in India alone, but all over the world?

This excruciating question could not but constantly trouble him—like a thorn in the spirit. It is surprising that hardly any of Iqbal's biographers, some of whom knew him intimately, have thrown any light on this problem which must have confronted Iqbal during the years of his maturity. For Iqbal was not insensitive; he was rarely complacent; and he could be self-critical. And such a person could not be unaware that between the thought and the act there was the shadow—or rather a void.

Iqbal was not, or at least did not think of himself, as contemplative. He could not be satisfied with a meditative approach to life. In his own way—an utterly impractical but passionately sincere way—he had wanted not merely to explain the world, but to change it. Thought that does not lead to action, Romain Rolland had observed, is a betrayal. This is a view which Iqbal fully endorsed. For him, too, the inward transformation of a man's being must, if it is real at all, find an objective correlative in the transformation of the external world. In what sense had his own life conformed to this criterion of judgment?

True, he had been a Professor of Philosophy. He had practised Law, though not with any conspicuous success. He had identified himself with the work of the Anjuman-i-Himayat Islam. At every annual session of this organization he had read poems; and these had never failed to move the well-to-do Muslim burghers of Lahore to contribute liberally to the funds of the Anjuman and feel virtuous after having done so. But, for the rest, he had kept rigorously outside the arena of practical struggle of his community; and as for the country, well, the idea had no longer any validity in his scheme of things. He had commented on events; he had criticized, often harshly, political and social trends; he had passed judgements on men and matters—and they were generally adverse and unflattering judgements. All this could be regarded as a legitimate and adequate function of a thinker and poet who wished to remain *au dessus de la melée*. But Iqbal had repudiated that kind of approach and detachment as unworthy and unheroic.

So the thorn in the spirit rankled. The void gaped before the inward eye of reflection. The thorn had to be extracted; the void had to be bridged. It was bridged, though not in the heroic manner one might have expected from one who had preached so heroic a message. There are, obviously, more things in heaven and earth than are dreamed of in one's philosophy; and unfortunately for man's self-esteem, they are more often than not petty and even ignoble things. The deeds that resulted from that immense exertion of the mind, that vast flight of the imagination, which we witnessed in the *Secrets of Self* and *Payam-i-Mashriq*, had about them the air of an anticlimax—and a somewhat humiliating anticlimax at that.

But let us not anticipate events. The problem of bringing Iqbal into more active public life had been worrying some of Iqbal's influential friends. Among these there was Sir Fazl-i-Hussain, the leader and one of the founders of the Unionist Party which represented the interests of the big and medium landlords, the squirearchy in fact, of the Punjab and which dominated the political life of the Province during the years between the two Wars. In 1924 Sir Fazl-i-Hussain and Iqbal were still on very freindly terms. We learn from the biography of his father by Azim Hussain that Sir Fazl-i-Husain urged Sir Malcolm Hailey (later Lord Hailey)—an astute British bureaucrat-politician who during his governorship of the Punjab played a decisive role in consolidating certain dynastic feudal interests as well as the position of the Unionist Party—to have Iqbal 'elevated to the Bench' of the Provincial High Court. This was one of the ways in which the British in India rewarded the loyalists, but it must be said to Iqbal's credit that, though he repeatedly came very near to it, he never wholly accepted the loyalist position. On this occasion, as on many others, he was indiscreet enough to speak out his mind. 'While the case was under consideration,' writes Azim Hussain, 'Dr Iqbal alienated the sympathies of officials by unrestrained criticism of the Government.' Sir Malcolm Hailey, who always entertained a somewhat exaggerated sense of his own importance and the importance of British prestige in India, did not recommend Iqbal for judgeship of the Punjab High Court.

But if the glory of the High Court judgeship was to be denied him, there were to be consolations two years later. For in 1926 Iqbal contested the election for the Provincial Legislative Council from the Lahore Muslim Constituency and was duly elected. In the past he had inveighed against the Councils and, indeed, ridiculed the whole absurd and fatuous apparatus of 'constitutional reforms'. He had accused those who put their faith in these devices of infantile make-believe, of begging. He had uncharitably criticized the Muslim deputation which had gone to London to explain the Indian Muslim viewpoint on the Khilafat question, charged it with 'ignorance of history' and added bravely:

> To Muslims unworthy is that kingship,
> Which is not bought with their own blood.

Yet, once again, when the temptation came his way he was unable to resist it. He had agreed to win his seat, not by his own blood, but by Muslim middle-class votes. In fairness to him, it must be added that he had been persuaded to enter the Legislative Council, much against his own inclination, by the pressure of his friends who felt that he would be more useful to the community by being a member of the Provincial Council. He had not done any begging for himself; all his begging had been done for him by his worthy and influential friends. But 'begging', even when done by proxy, and particularly when done by proxy, is not of the order of noble deeds in any philosophy, least of all in Iqbal's philosophy. For at this very moment he was writing:

> If I were to lose even one particle from the pattern
>     of my being,
> At that price I shall never accept immortality.

Immortality, of course, is another matter; it may be no more than a metaphor or it may be something immeasurably more than a metaphor. But membership of the Legislative Council was something very concrete and finite; and it could only be achieved by means of votes—and these had either to be bought or begged for. Iqbal after having abjured Western democracy—because it was trying to extract the thought of 'one man from the brain of two hundred donkeys'—was apparently quite agreeable to accept the benefices of what he knew to be sham democracy.

Thus the 'Chapter of Deeds' began in Iqbal's life with a deed which could by no stretch of imagination be described as an heroic deed. Even if one puts on it a most favourable complexion, it still appears to reflect a certain degree of opportunistic equivocation and ambivalence right at the very centre of will and purpose.

## A Chapter of Deeds

The ambivalence was to become accentuated in time; the opportunistic equivocations were to multiply with years. Each effort to bridge the gulf between the thought and the act was to make the contradiction between the ideal and the real more patent; each attempt to live his ideals was to lead him further and further down the velvet path of compromise; and each compromise was to be less noble, less justifiable, than its predecessor. And the thorn in the spirit was to rankle more and more as the full measure of this agonizing frustration was to be revealed to a mind never capable of wholly deceiving itself.

But this judgement must be qualified and certain attenuating circumstances must be taken into account. The fault is not always wholly of one's stars, nor always wholly one's own. In Iqbal's case the equivocation, the ambivalence, the compromises, the opportunism which made nonsense of the exalted principles he preached, were partly, perhaps even largely, the defects, not of and individual, but of a class and of a period. They could be traced back to the singularly unfortunate and unheroic historic position in which the Indian middle class—Hindu, Muslim, Sikh or of any other denomination—was placed. And Iqbal, after all, belonged to this class—a fact which, like most other eminent contemporaries, he tried to forget or evade by a thousand subtle subterfuges and sublimations.

Iqbal was a good student of early Islamic history; but he was not a good student of contemporary history and, therefore, was unable to understand fully his own predicament and the predicament of those whom he represented. He was unable to perceive the limitations of a colonial bourgeoisie; or rather, he was able to perceive them, but was not prepared to see them for what they were and tended to interpret them in terms of categories which had no reality. And it was a part of these limitations that Iqbal, and other eminent Indian public men of his time, could sincerely formulate the most altruistic ideals, think out the most impressive philosophies of disinterested action, spin out cerebral sublimities, and yet find it impossible to resist the most pitiable crumbs of material preferment which their masters dealt out to them. Iqbal did not see, or did not wish to see, that an everlasting equivocation and moral ambivalence was of the very essence of the destiny of the Indian middle class; that sooner or later, and sooner rather than later, even the most steadfast of idealists among its ranks were doomed to fall for the most trifling temptation; and that history had cruelly placed even the tragic nobility and heroism of self-denial and renunciation beyond their reach.

The membership of the Punjab Legislative Council was only the beginning. Iqbal's worthy and influential friends had also other plans for him so that he could fully utilize his various gifts for the advancement of his community, and incidentally, his own. Among these friends none was so influential, nor so tireless in his exertions to help Iqbal, as Sir Fazl-i-Hussain, the Unionist chief who could at least claim to be a super-mediocrity amongst the circus of political mediocrities which ran the Punjab. When in 1927 there was suggestion that a Muslim deputation should be sent to England to plead the Muslim case with the Secretary of State for India, in order that their interests should not go by default in the forthcoming reforms, Sir Fazl-i-Hussain 'asked Dr Iqbal to lead the deputation and collected Rs 3000 for the purpose'. 'This,' Azim Hussain tells us, 'would have assured a first-class political career for Dr Iqbal.'

Unfortunately, however, Iqbal was once again found wanting in 'tact'. It should be added that in this case it was financial and not diplomatic tact that was in question. The money collected by Sir Fazl-i-Hussain, was not considered adequate by Iqbal. 'He refused to go,' writes Azim Hussain, 'as it would have involved an expenditure of an extra few thousand rupees. Instead Choudhri Zafrulla Khan agreed to go, and assured a bright future for himself.' He did indeed: he was to become the Foreign Minister of Pakistan.

Sir Fazl-i-Hussain was indefatigable in his effort to see that Iqbal got on in life as he himself had so eminently got on. The estrangement between these two men which in 1935 was to lead to a public attack by Iqbal on his benefactor was still a thing of the future. Azim Hussain informs us: 'This did not deter Fazl-i-Hussain from making further efforts to help Dr Iqbal and he proposed that on the termination of Chaudhri Shahab-ud-Din's term as President of the Council, Dr Iqbal should be elected President with the support of the Unionist party.' Dr Iqbal once more

## A Chapter of Deeds

disappointed his well-wisher. He betrayed the same lack of discretion as he had done on an earlier occasion. Azim Hussain writes: 'Dr Iqbal, however, alienated the sympathies of the party by criticizing their policy and attacking them severely in the press, with the result that the majority of the Unionist Party refused to accept him as president.'

Nothing, however, deterred Sir Fazl-i-Hussain who was steadfast in his desire to help Iqbal, possibly because he was shrewd and sensible enough to realize that a word of approbation from Iqbal was worth more than all the sycophantic praise he received from the yes-men with whom he had surrounded himself. In 1931 he recommended Iqbal's name for nomination to the Second Round Table Conference. This time, fortunately, there was no impediment. Iqbal was duly nominated by the Viceroy, and he went to London in the fullness of time. But in London his tact once again failed him. He could not get on with the rest of the Muslim delegation. Worst of all, he quarrelled, Azim Hussain tells us, 'with Sir Akbar Hydari, a prominent member of the Muslim delegation. On his return to India he severely criticized the work of the Muslim delegation.' And, naturally, this criticism 'was greatly resented by the Secretary of State, because it belittled the proceedings of the Conference'.

It speaks a great deal for Sir Fazl-i-Hussain's devotion to Iqbal that, even after so exalted a personage as the Secretary of State for India had expressed disapproval of Iqbal's conduct, he should continue to champion the poet's cause with the authorities. If his son's testimony is to be believed, making allowance for a certain degree of filial special pleading, then it would appear that Sir Fazl-i-Hussain once again put up Iqbal's name for membership of the next Round Table Conference. Alternatively, he suggested that Iqbal might either be sent as one of the Indian delegation to the League of Nations or asked to serve on the Federal Structure Committee. The first recommendation was accepted and Iqbal was once again sent to attend the Round Table Conference. But once in London he had yet another fit of 'tactlessness' which permanently marred his prospects of 'a first-class political career', to use the significant phrase. While the Conference was in progress, remarks Azim Hussain, 'he resigned and returned to India, and denounced the British Government in the strongest possible terms in his address to the Muslim League'.

In point of fact the denunciation of the British Government which Iqbal had voiced in his address was by no means 'in the strongest possible terms'; it was mild in comparison to what quite a number of Congress leaders were indulging in; but it proved to be the last straw as far as the British Proconsul in India was concerned. Despite repeated urging by Sir Fazl-i-Hussain that Iqbal be given the sinecure post of membership of the Public Services Commission, the Viceroy was adamant in his refusal to countenance so recalcitrant a spirit as Iqbal in the bureaucratic hierarchy. Later, Sir Fazl-i-Hussain made another attempt: he put up Iqbal's name for choice as Indian Agent to South Africa. But it was unavailing.

Sir Fazl-i-Hussain's indulgence towards Iqbal was apparently unlimited; possibly he still hoped to get from Iqbal that word of approval which would have provided the Unionist leader with an authentic confirmation of his own political acumen. 'Having failed to secure a Government appointment for Dr Iqbal,' Azim Hussain goes on to say, 'Fazl-i-Hussain approached the Nizam of Hyderabad to help Dr Iqbal'. In reply Sir Akbar Hydari wrote: 'In reply to a wire to Iqbal asking him to wire definite extent and form of help, he has replied: "Five months' work, press, platform, interviews, party of five, rough estimate sixty thousand." Do you think I can ask my Committee and Government to shoulder such heavy expenditure?'

Obviously, Sir Akbar Hydari's task was impossible, with the Nizam feeling a pang at every penny that went out of the State Treasury. Sir Fazl-i-Hussain tried to smooth matters by suggesting a lower figure as to the sum to be spent and wrote: 'I think any assistance given to Dr Sir Mohammed Iqbal to take two or three good men with him, and to give interviews and lectures, will be most beneficial to the State, as well as Indian Muslims. I should like Hyderabad to accept the suggestion.' And the suggestion might have been accepted, but Iqbal 'insisted on his expensive proposal' and the Hyderabad Government was not prepared to pay the price.

Though by now some degree of coolness had developed between the Unionist leader and the Poet of Islam, Sir Fazl-i-Hussain, his son tells us, made one last attempt to help Iqbal. 'A similar effort,' he writes, 'was made three years later, when Fazl-i-Hussain wrote to Mian Amir-ud-din: "How is Iqbal? Sometime ago I heard he was not keeping well, and that he was in some difficulties.

I shall be glad if you will let me know, very confidentially, the exact position. I have been a great admirer of his since college days. I once more would like to make an effort to help him if I knew exactly how he stood, at present, in the matter of health and finances, and the real practice, if any, he has at present." Mian Amir-ud-din replied that Dr Iqbal had ceased to practice in 1931. His health was poor, and so were his finances. He suggested that if a series of lectures could be arranged at Hyderabad, and a substantial fee fixed, it would help him considerably. Fazl-i-Hussain prepared a scheme for the delivery of six lectures on 'Modern Islamic Thought' for a sum of Rs 10,000, but the Nizam's Government refused to agree to the terms proposed by Dr Iqbal, and negotiations failed again.'

No further attempts were made by Sir Fazl-i-Hussain to help Iqbal carve out a lucrative 'career' for himself. The relations between him and Iqbal had come to an open break. For at the annual meeting of the Anjuman-i-Himayat-Islam in 1935, Iqbal made a vitriolic attack on the Unionist chief, saying: 'It is really unfortunate that this rural–urban question [the Unionist Party claimed to represent the rural as opposed to urban interests] should have received the support of Sir Fazal-i-Hussain who obtained power, in the first instance, not as a rural leader but as a Muslim leader of the Province, but clung to his power by accentuating rural–urban differences. In this way, he secured as his colleagues some third-class men with no title to Government power, and the prestige and authority which the possession of such offices as ministerships secure, but who on that very account, viz., their mediocrity, look up to him as a superman. Some of the authorities also encouraged this policy as in this way they were able to break the force of the reforms of 1919. The result of these tendencies has been that so far as the Muslims are concerned, real leadership has stood at a distance, while the thoroughly incompetent "political adventurer" has come into the limelight.'

There is much in Iqbal's criticism of the Unionist Party's politics—based on a most unsavoury mixture of demagogy, opportunism, nepotism and 'loyalism'—which is just and unchallengeable, though it lends itself to the counter-charge that Iqbal by voicing this criticism was merely trying to rationalize his own failure to take advantage of the opportunities offered him of securing the plums of office. That, however, is not really the issue involved in the revealing episode of the relationship between Sir Fazl-i-Hussain and Iqbal; the personal aspect of the question is merely incidental and unimportant, and the fact that it has received some prominence is indicative of the comparatively rudimentary level at which politics in India has moved during the past few decades. The real point at issue is the validity or otherwise of Iqbal's philosophy of polity. His failure to vindicate and justify it in practice, to fulfil himself in the sphere of action which he had chosen for himself, cannot but raise serious questions as to the adequacy of his conceptions and his understanding of politics.

Azim Hussain, while justifying his father who at least had the virtue of being successful, explains Iqbal's failure by saying: 'The truth of the matter was that Dr Iqbal was not a politician; he was a political philosopher. He was an idealist, and could not understand that politics was a game of compromise. He failed to get office, or become a leader, because he was more of a poet, and a thinker, than a man of affairs.' Other, more admiring biographers of Iqbal have offered similar explanations and in terms even more flattering to their hero. But, in fact, these explanations are simply statements of the problem in different words. They are unsatisfying and superficial attempts to make virtue of a failure. At best they are based on half-truths.

For the fact must be faced that Iqbal was not an adolescent *ingénu* when he decided to enter the arena of active political life. He was a man of ripe age; over fifty in fact. He could not have been unaware of the conditions in which the political game was being played in the Punjab—and in India generally. As a politician, therefore, he could not expect any preferential treatment. He had to play the game according to the rules of corruption—and corruption has its rules—which prevailed around him. His success and failure, he must have, or at least ought to have, known would depend on his capacity to manipulate the political machinery of which he had agreed to become a part. He could not justifiably present the fact of his being a poet and thinker, or 'a political philosopher', as an alibi for his failure. For he recognized no such division of personality, no duality between idea and action.

The failure of Iqbal may well have been due to his being at once too much of an 'idealist' and not being idealistic enough. He was too much of an 'idealist' in the sense that, though he was prepared to play politics, he invariably recoiled from some of its more obvious deceptions and insincerities and was not prepared to submit to its imperatives. And he was not idealistic enough in the sense that, although he repudiated the whole basis and concept of Western bourgeois democracy in his political philosophy, in practice his mind was still dominated by the very ideas, values, and even the irrelevancies of that form of polity. It is startling, for instance, to learn from Iqbal himself that he took 'the reforms of 1919' seriously: at the time when they were first announced he had, quite rightly, ridiculed them as worthless. What had happened to change his valuation between 1919 and 1926 when he first decided to contest the election to the Provincial Legislative Council? Iqbal does not tell us, nor do any of his hero-worshipping biographers. It is no less baffling to find him serving on the Round Table Conference. He could not have been so ignorant as to believe that the Muslim delegation—or for that matter any other delegation—had gone to London for any other purpose than 'begging' in his sense of the term. The man who would not 'beg' for eternal life was prepared to associate himself with those who were begging, and in the most craven fashion, for percentages, weightages, representation. True, the association was short-lived; but his motives for breaking the association will always lend themselves to varying interpretations. Iqbal in the *Payam* had described the League of Nations as a 'Society of Coffin-Thieves'. Yet, apparently, he would have had no objection to participating in the deliberations of these 'Coffin-Thieves', if only the Viceroy had been agreeable to his nomination as a member of the Indian delegation. Finally, there is something humiliating to see him haggling with the miserly potentate of Hyderabad over the fee for his lectures on 'Islamic Thought'. For what was this haggling but a manifestation of the shopkeepers' mentality which he denounced so loudly and so vehemently?

But the inventory of these dismal contradictions between the thought and the act could be indefinitely prolonged if our purpose were to show Iqbal's inconsistencies. That is not the purpose since the point at issue is something bigger even than Iqbal's personality: it is a whole political philosophy, a theory of social action which is involved in this fiasco. The theory may be called the 'Men of Good Will Theory'. It is a theory which finds expression repeatedly in historical experience. From Plato down to H. G. Wells and Iqbal himself, intellectuals of varying stature have been inclined to believe that all that is needed to end the ills of the world is to put the right people in the right places; to have the society and all its functions regulated by a disinterested class of intellectual *Samurai*, as it were; and place the Government in the hands of saints and martyrs who should rule, not from the 'tomb' as Eliot has it in his *Murder in the Cathedral*, but from the Council Chamber.

Iqbal in his own way, determined by his background and upbringing, fully shared this naive and pathetic political illusion. We, therefore, find him lamenting the machinations of opportunistic politicians, charging others with being mediocre political adventurers, because they would not accept his advice and guidance. But he made no attempt to understand the defects of the polity with which he had to deal, to relate them to the social order in which they had their origin. His critique of politics, for all its invocation of exalted principles, never went far enough to see in the disorder and discontent of our time anything more than personal perversities of this or that individual politician or the defaults of this or that political institution. He thus mistook the symptoms for the cause of the disease and in so doing placed himself on the same level as those whose shallow understanding of social and political phenomena he criticized. To go beyond this rudimentary analysis of the world in which he lived, he would have had to allow his thought to break out of the narrow categories of which it was a prisoner, but he was too much in love with his prison to allow that to happen.

The tragedy of Iqbal as a man of action and a politician was not that he failed in achieving his purpose. That can happen to even the most clairvoyant of revolutionaries and political prophets. The tragedy of Iqbal was that he failed to understand fully the extent, the nature and the cause of his failure. For this signified an irreducible misconception right at the very core of his vision. And it was the realization that this misconception was there and could not be removed—a realization which he tried in a thousand ways to rationalize or suppress—that accounts for the note of frustration which is the constant undertone of his poetry written during his mature phase. For this was the thorn in the spirit.

CHAPTER VIII

## The Dead Sea Fruit

At this point there is bound to be a chorus of dissentient voices. They can legitimately protest that it is manifestly absurd to suggest that Iqbal failed to vindicate his political philosophy in the field of action. After all, it has been claimed and will continue to be claimed, that Iqbal's philosophy of polity has borne visible fruit in the creation of a new nation and a new State—Pakistan.

The issue is clouded with so many passions and so many prejudices that it is doubtful if it will ever be discussed dispassionately by our generation. This is as true of the champions of Pakistan as those who are opposed to it. But in a biography of Iqbal we are bound to make some attempt to get the facts of the case in some sort of a perspective. How far can Iqbal be regarded as the author and creator of the Pakistan conception? How far did he materially help in building up the political movement which was to lead to the birth of Pakistan?

These are controversial questions, but they must be answered. The first thing is to get the facts clear. Before 1930 Pakistan was not even a name or, if it was, nobody had heard of it in public. In that year Iqbal presided at the annual session of the All-India Muslim League held in Allahabad. As is customary on such occasion, he read a lengthy address at the opening session in which he made a *tour de horizon* of the general political situation in the country with specific attention to the problem of Muslim interests. But his address is somewhat different from the usual generalities and platitudes which are the stock-in-trade of presidential addresses. It has a seriousness, an intellectual gravity, and a dignity which never failed him when he really directed his mind to any particular problem. There is a good deal in it that is parochial and polemical, but it also has passage of—for an Indian gathering—remarkably lucid prose.

He begins by denying that he has any special political axe to grind:

> I lead no party; I follow no leader. I have given the best part of my life to a careful study of Islam, its law and polity, its culture, its history and literature. This constant contact with the Spirit of Islam, as it unfolds itself in time, has, I think, given me a kind of insight into its significance as a world-fact. It is in the light of this insight, whatever its value, that, while assuming that the Muslims of India, are determined to remain true to the Spirit of Islam, I propose, not to guide you in your decisions, but to attempt the humbler task of bringing clearly to your consciousness the main principle which, in my opinion, should determine the general character of those decisions.

He then proceeds to develop the argument so dear to his heart regarding the true nature of Islam. It is not, he contends just another religion among many religions, but a unique world-view embracing the whole sphere of human activity; a total philosophy if you like, which cannot be reconciled with narrow nationalistic ideals. It differs, moreover, from other religions, like Christianity, for example, in that it is not other-worldly, but accepts the world of time and space and believes in a Kingdom that is of the earth. As the whole argument is fundamental to Iqbal's position and is here stated with greater clarity than anywhere else by him, it deserves to be quoted at some length:

> It cannot be denied that Islam, regarded as an ethical ideal plus a certain kind of polity—by which expression I mean a social structure, regulated by a legal system and animated by a specific ethical ideal—has been the chief formative factor in the life-history of the Muslims of India. It has furnished those basic emotions and loyalties which gradually unify scattered individuals and groups, and finally transform them into a well-defined people, possessing a moral consciousness of their own. Indeed it is no exaggeration to suggest that India is perhaps the only country where Islam, as a people-

building force, has worked at its best. In India, as elsewhere, the structure of Islam as a society is almost entirely due to the working of Islam as a culture inspired by a specific ethical ideal. What I mean to say is that Muslim society, with its remarkable homogeneity and inner unity, has grown to be what it is, under the pressure of the laws and institutions associated with the culture of Islam.

The ideas set free by European political thinking however, are now rapidly changing the outlook of the present generation of Muslims both in India and outside India. Our younger men inspired by these ideas, are anxious to see them as living force in their own countries, without any critical appreciation of the facts which have determined their evolution in Europe. In Europe Christianity was understood to be a purely monastic order which gradually developed into a church-organization. The protest of Luther was directed against the church-organization, not against any system of polity of a secular nature, for the obvious reason that there was no such polity associated with Christianity. And Luther was perfectly justified in rising in revolt against this organization, though, I think, he did not realize that in the peculiar condition which obtained in Europe, his revolt would eventually mean the displacement of the universal ethics of Jesus by the growth of a plurality of national and hence narrower systems of ethics. Thus the upshot of the intellectual movement initiated by such men as Luther and Rousseau was the break-up of the One into a mutually ill-adjusted many, the transformation of a human into a national outlook, requiring a more realistic foundation, such as the notion of country, and finding expression through varying systems of polity evolved on national lines, on lines which recognize territory as the only principle of political solidarity.

...The universal ethics of Jesus is displaced by national systems of polity and ethics. The conclusion to which Europe is consequently driven is that religion is a private affair of the individual and has nothing to do with what is called man's temporal life. Islam does not bifurcate the unity of man into an irreconcilable duality of spirit and matter. In Islam God and the universe, spirit and matter, church and state, are organic to each other. Man is not the citizen of a profane world to be renounced in the interests of a world of spirit situated elsewhere. To Islam matter is spirit realizing itself in space and time... A Luther in the world of Islam is an impossible phenomenon; for here there is no Church-organization, similar to that of Christianity in the Middle Ages, inviting a destroyer. In the world of Islam we have a universal polity whose fundamentals are believed to have been revealed, but whose structure, owing to our legists' want of contact with the modern world, stands today in need of renewed power by fresh adjustments. I do not know what will be the final fate of the national idea in the world of Islam. Whether Islam will assimilate and transform it, as it has transformed and assimilated before many ideas expressive of a different spirit, or allow a radical transformation of its own structure by the force of this idea, is hard to predict... At the present moment the national idea is racializing the outlook of Muslims, and thus materially counteracting the humanizing task of Islam... I hope you will pardon me for this apparently academic discussion. To address this session of the All-India Muslim League you have selected a man who has not despaired of Islam as a living force for freeing the outlook of men from its geographical limitations, who believes that religion is a power of the utmost importance in the life of individuals as well as states, and finally who believes that Islam is itself Destiny and will not suffer a destiny...

After this bold declaration, Iqbal descends to more mundane regions—to the problem of reconciling the various groups and their interests in India. He repeats the unexceptionable platitude that 'the unity of an Indian nation, therefore, must be sought, not in the negation, but in the mutual harmony and co-operation of the many... And it is on the discovery of Indian unity in this direction that the fate of India as well as of Asia really depends...'

But why has it been impossible to discover this principle of harmony and co-operation? Iqbal has his diagnosis; not a very brilliant diagnosis, but certainly a revealing one. We have failed because, he observes, 'we suspect each other's intentions and inwardly aim at dominating each other. Perhaps in the higher interests of mutual co-operation we cannot afford to part *with monopolies which circumstances have placed in our hands...* (italics are mine)'. The passage is significant. After the sublime flight into the sphere of the ideals of Islam which is 'a Destiny and will not suffer a destiny' we are pulled down by the force of gravity into the not so heroic realm of economic exigencies. The real reason why Indian unity has been impossible to achieve, according to Iqbal, is because certain groups (presumably, the Hindus) having established monopolies in various economic fields are not prepared to share them with their Muslim counterparts. This is not a very original analysis of the origin of Hindu–Muslim conflict in India, though it happens within limits, to be a correct analysis. It might have been furnished by any mediocre middle-class politician. But coming from the Poet of Islam it has a unique significance. In his 'Warning to the West' he had taken Westerners to task for treating God's earth as 'a shop'. Now he acknowledges, by implication which cannot be mistaken, that the 'shop' is important, even that it is the heart of the matter. He does more. He enters the 'shop', though with the most idealistic flourishes. He is prepared to do business, provided it is given another name less redolent of the unsavoury odour of the market-place.

Iqbal goes on to affirm his optimism about the possibility of harmonizing the discordancies of Indian polity. He offers a demagogic defence of what he terms 'Communalism': 'There are communalisms and communalisms...Communalism, in its higher aspect, then, is indispensable to the formation of a harmonious whole in a country like India.' And he endorses what he describes as 'the Muslim demand for the creation of a Muslim India'; and he would like the house to endorse it with all the emphasis at its command. Always bolder than others, he goes further:

> Personally I would go even further. I would like to see the Punjab, North-West Frontier Province, Sind and Baluchistan amalgamated into a single state. Self-government within the British Empire, or without the

> British Empire, and the formation of a consolidated North-West Indian Muslim state appears to me to be the final destiny of the Muslims at least of North-West India.... The proposal was put forward before the Nehru Committee. They rejected it on the ground that, if carried into effect, it would give a very unwieldly state. This is true so far as the area is concerned; in point of population the state contemplated by the proposal would be much less than some of the present Indian provinces. The exclusion of Ambala Division and perhaps some districts where non-Muslims predominate, will make it less extensive and more Muslim in population—so that the exclusion suggested will enable this consolidated state to give a more effective protection to non-Muslim minorities within its area.

He assures the Hindus and the British that this administrative and political reorganization of India is really in their interests:

> The idea need not alarm the Hindus or the British. India is the greatest Muslim country in the world. The Life of Islam as a cultural force in this living country very largely depends on its centralization in a specified territory. This centralization of the most living portion of the Muslims of India whose military and police service has, notwithstanding unfair treatment from the British, made the British rule possible in this country, will eventually solve the problem of India as well as of Asia. It will intensify their sense of responsibility and deepen their patriotic feeling. Thus, possessing full opportunity of development within the body-politic of India, the North-West Indian Muslims will prove the best defenders of India against a foreign invasion, be that invasion one of ideas [an amiable reference to the danger of Communism] or bayonets... I therefore demand the formation of a consolidated Muslim State in the best interests of India and Islam. For India it means security and peace resulting from an internal balance of power; for Islam an opportunity to rid itself of the stamp that Arabian Imperialism was forced to give it, to mobilize its laws, its education, its

culture and to bring them into closer contact with its own original spirit and with the spirit of modern times...

There is no need to quote any more. Here we have the crux of the argument; the seed, which, it is claimed, was to grow up and bear fruit in the shape of Pakistan. How far is this claim valid? How far is it possible to relate the fruit to the seed?

A number of things must be noted. In Iqbal's scheme for a 'Muslim India', it is still not a question of a separate State. 'Muslim India' is still seen as an integral part of India, functioning 'within the body-politic of India'. Indeed, it would be more accurate to describe his scheme as a scheme for clear demarcation of 'Spheres of Influence'—or 'Sphere of Exploitation'—for the Hindu and Muslim bourgeoisie of India. In one part the Muslims could have profitable monopolies; in the others Hindus could enjoy their economic supremacy. It was to be a sharing of the spoils. There is no mention here of an 'Eastern Pakistan'; and one is justified in assuming that Iqbal did not trouble himself about the Muslims of eastern Bengal, possibly because he did not regard them, to use his phrase, part of 'the most living portion of the Muslims in India'. Most important of all, the term 'Pakistan' is scrupulously, and possibly deliberately, avoided.

It might be that Iqbal at this stage had not made up his own mind on the subject and the notion was still somewhat hazy and undefined. The late Edward Thompson, for instance, has left it on record that in the course of a conversation with Iqbal, the latter admitted to him that, although he had championed a scheme for Muslim India, he did not believe it to be in the interests either of India as a whole or of the Muslim community. 'Disastrous', in fact, is the term which he is supposed to have used. But such private conversations can only be accepted as valid evidence if there is authentic objective or documentary verification available. Is there such testimony available?

The answer is, to some extent, yes.[1] It is undoubtedly significant that Iqbal made no serious effort to put forward his scheme at the Round Table Conference in London. It is true he resigned from it in disgust, but that had little to do with his scheme. Pakistan, it is

---

[1] See the Preface to this edition.

reasonable to suggest, was not yet even a bargaining counter which the Muslim leadership was prepared to bring forward in order to get certain other, more moderate demands accepted by the Hindu leadership. It was still dismissed as an unpractical and crazy 'Undergraduates Scheme'. Two years after his Presidential address to the All-India Muslim League, Iqbal was asked to preside at the All-India Muslim Conference held at Lahore in the summer of 1932. Iqbal in his address to this body did not make any specific reference to his earlier blueprint for a North-West Muslim State in India. He merely posed the problem of Hindu–Muslim concord in rather general and decidedly hopeful terms:

> In view of the visible and invisible points of contact between the various communities of India I do believe in the possibility of constructing a harmonious whole, whose unity cannot be disturbed by the rich diversity which it must carry within its bosom. The problem of ancient Indian thought was how the One became many without sacrificing its oneness. Today the problem has come down from its heights to the grosser plane of our political life, and we have to solve it in its inverse from, i.e. how the many can become One without sacrificing its plural character...

The vagueness of this observation could not but have been purposive. For Iqbal was not normally fond of obliquity of statement. In this case, one would be correct in supposing that it was meant to leave the door open for negotiation on a basis even less separatist in implication than the earlier Muslim demand. There is some reason to believe that Iqbal did not deviate any further towards separation beyond the position he took up in 1930. As late as June 21 1937, less than a year before his death, in a letter to Jinnah he suggested no more than 'a redistribution of the country on the lines of racial, religious, and linguistic affinities' It is relevant that he avoided the use of the term 'division'.

There is thus considerable justification in the suggestion that Iqbal in his lifetime never wholly embraced the Pakistan idea. But it is only honest to add that this does not mean that his personality and writings did not contribute towards the creation of Pakistan. They certainly did. His fervent idealization of Islam, not merely as a religion, but as a comprehensive polity exercised a very far-reaching restraining influence upon the Muslim intelligentsia. Together with a number of other factors of an economic character, it served to stem the development of a secular outlook among the Muslim youth. His ardent Pan-Islamic fantasies fired the youthful Muslim imagination with a new complex of dream-fulfilments. Even those among them who had previously been groping towards socialistic thought, now were drawn towards another ideal—far more tempting because far less rational; some of them even began to give their socialism a Pan-Islamic orientation. Cumulatively, Iqbal by his poetry, by his political and philosophical writings, succeeded in creating an ambient and infectious mood of irrational, revivalistic fervour in which the Pakistan idea could grow and come to its fruition.

Nor is that all. There is no doubt that in the last few years of his life he exerted his influence to strengthen the Muslim League as a political organization. In his Presidential address to its Allahabad session in 1930 he had lamented 'our disorganized condition' which 'has already confused political issues vital to the life of the community'; and he had added: 'The present crisis in the history of India demands complete organization and unity of will and purpose in the Muslim community, both in your own interest and the interest of India as a whole.' When Jinnah visited Lahore to reorganize the Muslim League, which was the weakest in the Punjab owing to the Unionist Party's domination of political life, Iqbal, although keeping very indifferent health, helped the founder and creator of Pakistan in his task.

There is, indeed, little doubt that during this last phase Iqbal was drawn into closer association with Jinnah. True, he was not greatly impressed by the latter's understanding of Islam, its ideals and its polity. There is even some reason to believe that though he gave Jinnah his political support, he maintained an attitude of reserve towards him. It is pertinent in this connection to relate an episode towards the end of his life. Iqbal, though he had a controversy over the Qadiani question with Jawaharlal Nehru—a controversy in which Iqbal was, incidentally, on much firmer historical grounds than Nehru—entertained very warm feelings for the man who, after all, despite never having accepted the religion of 'the Book', was his kin. When Nehru was in Lahore, Iqbal expressed a desire to meet him. In his *Discovery of India*, Nehru writes:

A few months before his death, as he lay on his sickbed, he sent for me and I gladly obeyed the summons. As I talked to him about many things I felt that, in spite of differences, how much we had in common and how easy it would be to get on with him. He was in reminiscent mood and he wandered from one subject to another, and I listened to him, talking little myself. I admired him and his poetry and it pleased me greatly to feel that he liked me and had a good opinion of me. A little before I left him he said to me: 'What is there in common between Jinnah and you? He is a politician, you are a patriot'.

This attitude of reserve notwithstanding, Iqbal had probably greater regard and esteem for Jinnah than for most of his Muslim contemporaries. He may or may not have followed him in everything, but he was a sufficiently good judge of human character to realize that here was a man who, whatever his failings and defects, was steadfast in purpose, possessed an indomitable will, and was above those petty, opportunistic considerations which dominated the outlook of the mediocre 'political adventurer' with whom he had to deal all his life in the Punjab. He could rely upon Jinnah which he could not upon other eminent Muslim politicians. Had he lived longer, the association between these two men would almost certainly have ripened into firmer bonds of political co-operation.

Finally, there is the movement of events and the pressure of that movement has to be considered. Iqbal was not, despite all his claims to the detachment of an intellectual who led 'no party and followed no leader', impervious to this pressure. Pakistan was not a practical and realizable objective in 1935, but it had become an inevitability in 1945. The mood of the Muslim intelligentsia had changed; and the mood had changed because its circumstances had changed. During the war years the Muslim middle class had vastly strengthened its material position; it was better organized; and this organizational strength and confidence, combined with certain other external factors and the British patronage, had placed it in a position to fight for and get its pound of flesh. Moreover, the predominantly Hindu leadership of the Congress, with its narrow sectarian outlook, its gross ignorance of any but the British constitutional parallels, and its incredible lack of imagination and understanding in dealing with the legitimate demands of the Muslims, had thrown even those Muslim intellectuals who were by no means enamoured of the Pakistan idea, into the arms of the Muslim League. It is highly doubtful if Iqbal would have been able to keep a stable judgment and sane outlook during the years of political insanity which culminated in the division of India and the tragedy of the Punjab.

It would have been impossible for him to do so. Iqbal always reflected the moods of his community; he often anticipated these moods. The probability, therefore, is that, had Iqbal lived another ten years, he would have championed Pakistan with an ecstatic fanaticism. It would have presented itself to him as the very destiny which he had been striving to create for Muslim India. He would have seen in it the crowning achievements of his life, the practical vindication of his philosophy, the power and the glory of his message, the potential Kingdom of God on earth.

And in a superficial sense he would have been right. But only in a superficial sense. For in a deeper sense the question would have remained unanswered. How far did the fruit partake of the nature of the seed? And did not the fruit, in the very moment of its ripeness, turn into the Dead Sea Fruit? These questions would still have rankled in the mind, like the eternal thorn in the spirit.

For they are serious, fundamental. No serious and honest analysis can avoid the conclusion that the creation of Pakistan represents the negation of those very ideals of polity which Iqbal was so vehemently supposed to champion. True, because of an irreducible opaqueness in his thinking, he found nothing contradictory and inconsistent in declaring at one and the same time that '...the piece of earth with which the spirit of man happens to be temporarily associated' did not matter at all; that Islam rejected the ideal of national and territorial loyalty as the basis for political solidarity; and yet go on to suggest that 'the life of Islam as a cultural force in this living country very largely depends on its centralization in a specified territory'. But the contradiction and inconsistency are there none the less.

There is more here, in fact, than just a contradiction and inconsistency. There is self-deception, unconscious, subtle, but unmistakable self-deception. This applies both to Iqbal in so far as he associated himself with the Pakistan demand, and to those who turn to Iqbal's philosophy for an ideological justification of Pakistan. The underlying argument in the case of both is crudely demagogic, though it might be phrased in the most glittering language of idealism. If the remark which Iqbal puts into Tarik's mouth—that 'every country is our country because it is the country of our God'—means what it says, then the demand for the association of Indian Muslims 'with a specified territory' and the carving out from India of a 'Muslim State' is absurd, demagogic, and contrary to the ideals of Islamic polity. If the remark is a mere rhetorical figure of speech, then Islamic polity must be judged on the same basis and in the same terms as other systems of polity. And if it is so judged, it would be obvious that the birth of Pakistan is not the Spirit of Islam working on matter, but matter working on the Spirit of Islam and transforming it radically in the process.

That is the heart of the paradox. Though it is now customary and conventional to refer to Iqbal as the Philosopher and Poet of Pakistan, the Pakistan idea in its materialization represents the absolute refutation of the very basis of Iqbal's political philosophy. For its origin and its development is initiated and actuated by the same kind of motives which led to the Reformation, the break-up of Christendom, and the rise of national states in Europe. There are important differences of detail no doubt, due to the distorted growth of a capitalist economy under the stultifying compulsions and limitations created by colonial rule which has modified the character of normal transition from a feudal to bourgeois society. But the essential inner pattern is identical. 'A Luther in the world of Islam, however, is an impossible phenomenon' Iqbal tried to comfort his bemused Muslim congregation at Allahabad. Really? Future historians may yet come to recognize in Iqbal himself the Luther of Islam, a Luther turned inside out, but still a Luther.

CHAPTER IX

## The Book of Eternity

A man's life is lived simultaneously at a variety of levels. The unitary conception of individuality is largely illusory; the individual is rarely, if ever, individual. The human personality is a plurality, a many in one: it is not a monolithic structure and of a piece, but is made up of a series of layers, of strata, of disparate and even contradictory elements of being, held together by the most tenuous threads and encased in a parchment shell which is also a mask. This makes the task of biography one of considerable difficulty. For convention demands a consecutive chronological narrative; but such a narrative falsifies the complex and tangled pattern of life and gives one a deceptive simulacrum, not the multi-dimensional living reality. The problem is how to combine the two different sets of perspectives, the perspective of time and the perspective of experience.

And it is not easy to achieve this dual focus. For the effort to do so may, and often does, result in a confusion of vision, leading to a kind of mental parallax. The experience at the different levels of being, moreover, admits of infinite shades, nuances and variations. All that may be negative at one level may well appear as positive at another. Thus a man may be involved in all manner of failures, absurdities, even heart-breaking frustrations and yet at the same time he may be realizing the most luminous of fulfilments; or, inversely, he may on the surface be eminently successful, full of achievement and perfections, and yet his inner life may be an utter fiasco and desolation.

Iqbal's life is illustrative of this duality. By common consent the ten years between 1924 and 1934 were the most active years of his career. He had come out of the ivory tower and was taking part in public life, and particularly, in Muslim politics. The part he took was intermittent, but it was nevertheless important. It was during these ten years that he got himself elected to the Provincial Legislative Council, presided at a session of the Muslim League and at another of the Muslim Conference, attended the Round Table Conference and revisited Europe. Even his most uncritical admirers have not suggested that he achieved any singular success in politics or that his attempts to guide the destinies of his co-religionists were conspicuously effective. As a practical man of action, in spite of his philosophy of action, he was a failure; and he himself recognized this failure tacitly when he withdrew from active politics, partly because of his health, but also out of disgust.

Yet this period of almost unredeemed disappointment and even humiliating frustrations on the material plane was, in some ways, the richest and most fruitful phrase of his career. During these ten years he produced three major books of verse and of prose. Two of the books of verse are in Persian; one is in Urdu. The prose work is written in English. But though they differ in form and in language, they all have one attribute in common. They are works which will endure and probably outlast our time. To have produced so much excellence in so short and trying a period is no mean achievement by any standards of human judgment.

The axiom already stated bears repetition. We make poetry out of quarrels with ourselves and our quarrels with the world in which we live. And we make philosophy, too, out of the same stuff. This is, perhaps, only another way of saying that in the crucible of imagination the raw material of experience is transformed, or rather transmuted, into the pure gold of perception. That is the function of imagination and Iqbal had abundant gifts of imagination. In the poetry written during these ten years we are not spared the quarrels which he had with himself and with the world. They are all there. So are the disappointments, dejections, and even exasperations of a man out of sympathy with his times and yet being driven by the strong tides of history, inexorably, almost without realizing it, on and on in a direction which he did not desire. There is a sense of frustration, too deep for tears. And above all a feeling of inner loneliness of the spirit, for Iqbal by now had despaired of finding the compassionate friend 'who knows the ways of ministering to the heart'.

But something has happened. All the tangled stuff of experience has suffered a sea change. The endless and exhausting quarrels with himself and with the world have somehow acquired the quality of the serene ecstacy of reconciliation. The dejections, the disappointments and exasperation have been transformed into exultations. The sense of despair and frustration has almost become a sense of fulfilment which is beyond despair. The ineluctable solitude carries with it the promise of an ultimate communion with something that is and is not. By what strange process of alchemy has all this occurred? We do not know. But the fact that it has occurred is not in doubt: And the fact is important.

First, in the chronological sequence comes a collection of Persian verse called *Zabur-i-Ajam* (Psalms of the East). It is formally very miscellaneous and was published in June 1927, during the 'parliamentary phase' of Iqbal's career. In its first part, from which the book derives its title, Iqbal uses practically every formal pattern known to Persian poetry—ghazals, couplets, quatrains. But the ghazals predominate. The second part consists of a long poem in the form of question and answer and is called 'The New Garden of Mystery'.[1] The last part is entitled 'The Book of Bondage'.

It is, however, the 'Psalms of the East' which constitute the most important part of the collection. There is redundancy and repetition in these 'Psalms' which no Persian poet, not even Rumi, was able altogether to avoid, and of which Iqbal certainly was never able wholly to steer clear. There are also, as always with Iqbal, lapses into an irritating turgidity of expression. Yet these defects of redundancy, repetitiveness and turgidity are less noticeable in the *Zabur* than almost any other work of Iqbal. For the most part the stream of poetry flows with a delightful limpidness; there is depth and there is transparency. The vision is nowhere out of focus; the perception has a crystalline purity; the articulation seldom strikes a note of artifice and involution of expression.

Iqbal is, of course, still anxious to preach his peculiar message, but somehow the solemnity of the pulpit has been forgotten. Instead, there is lightness of the spirit, the tone has grace, and the message rarely ceases to be a song. He seems to have thrown

[1] Written in answer to a well-known mystical work by Mahmud Shabistvi, *The Garden of Mystery*.

overboard much of the didactic ballast, the heavy homiletics, which weighted down the wings of inspiration in the *Asrar* and *Ramuz* and prevented it from soaring. The lyrical impulse has returned—it had never been wholly absent—but at a higher level of apprehension. We are no longer confronted with adolescent moods overcharged with significances which they could not sustain, but with the mirror of adult experience, and the significances are never laboured because they are self-evident and manifest. And, as always with Iqbal, there is melody and music. And what a melody and what a music!

But, first, let us state the theme. It is very simple, so simple as to sound sentimental. Yet there is very little trace of sentimentality in the 'Psalms' in the original and no attempt to overplay the pathetic note, even if it is difficult to avoid a touch of sentimentality in the translation. Iqbal states the main theme himself in his admonition to the reader at the beginning of the *Zabur*:

> Very far and wide is the valley of love,
> But there are times when the journey of a hundred years,
> is completed in the duration of a sigh.
> Be lost in your search
> And never abandon hope,
> For that, too, is wealth which is sometimes found
> by the wayside.

There are other motifs and other themes; there is a certain amount of polemics—polemics not only with the world, but also with God. But these are of relatively minor consequence. What is really important is the theme of the human heart and its ardent pilgrimage through the valley of love. But the heart whose pilgrimage we are allowed to follow is no ordinary heart. It is passionate; it is compassionate; it is infinitely alert and sensitive. The *Zabur* begins with the poet's prayer:

> Lord, grant me a heart that is aware of itself,
> Grant me a vision which can see the intoxication in
> the wine.

And this prayer is repeated later in the book in slightly different words:

> Grant, Oh Grant that heart
> All whose ecstacies
> Are from its own wine.
>
> Take, Oh Take, this heart away,
> Which is lost to itself,
> And is alien to thought.

The pilgrimage, therefore, acquires the quality of an endless apocalypse. The depths of the human heart are laid bare—but in a manner very different from that of Restif's *Monsieur Nicolas*. The theme enables Iqbal to modulate through the whole gamut of human experience—and beyond. There is ecstasy in the Psalms; and there is the stillness of deep thought. There is passion; and there is the serenity of an awareness that is beyond passion. There is a sense of joy; and there is despair. There is doubt; and there is certitude. There is the solitude of a heart whose longings are at once too vast and too exigent for any human intimacy to satisfy; and there is a sense of ineffable communion. And above all, and inevitably, there is the compulsion of love—love sacred and love profane. But the terms, in the moment of intense realization, become interchangeable; the barriers are no more; and the categories are no longer exclusive but complementary—and even inclusive. Here, for example, is love which can express itself only through the symbols which are of the earth and of the flesh:

> Remember the days when we drank,
> To the music of the harp and the flute,
> The cup of wine was in my hand,
> And the flask was held in his (or hers).

And, below, we have a love which needs no symbols from the world of time and space to communicate itself because it is beyond time and space:

> In one word
> I could have uttered
> The longings of the whole world.
> But I so loved your presence
> That I gave my story at length.

But how is one to measure the ecstacy of one against the ecstasy of the other? For, in the last analysis, both are beyond measure.

And so the pilgrimage continues, without end. At each step the heart is awakened, its depths are stirred, the awareness tries to outreach its limits. But with each new awakening, each new effort of the awareness, the horizon recedes. The burden of the mystery remains. The awful searching questions which have haunted the spirit of man ever since the beginning of time continue to urge the pilgrim onwards in his quest:

> From what source are you?
> And from what place?
> That the azure sky has drawn
> Across your path a thousand eyes
> With stars.

Thus Iqbal poses the everlasting question. Surely, he says, there must be some goal, some tangible objective, to a journey which has required so vast a cosmic preparation. Surely, he hints, there must be a destiny beyond the dust:

> This I understand
> That the world is dust
> And we are but a handful of dust.
> But from whence comes the ache of seeking
> In every particle of our being?

And in 'The New Garden of Mystery' Iqbal tries to furnish an answer to this question of questions. It is not a new answer. For he had already given it in the *Asrar*. Only now it has acquired even greater clarity and precision:

> If you say that the 'I' is a mere illusion
> An appearance among other appearances.
> Then tell me who is the subject of this illusion?
> Look within and discover
> The world is visible;
> Yet its existence needs proof!
> Not even the intellect of an angel can comprehend it.
> The 'I' is invisible and needs no proof!
> Think awhile and see thine own secret;
> The 'I' is Truth; it is no illusion;
> When it ripens, it becomes eternal.
> Lovers, even though separated from the beloved live

> in blissful union.
> It is possible to give wings to a mere spark
> And make it flutter for ever and ever.
> The eternity of God is elemental and not the
> reward of His action,
> That eternity is superior which a borrowed soul
> Wins for herself by love's frenzy.
> Why fear that death which comes from without,
> For when the 'I' ripens into a self,
> It has no danger of dissolution.
> There is a more subtle death which makes me
> tremble!
> This death is falling from true love's frenzy.
> Saving one's spark and not giving it freely to the
> heaps of chaff.
> Cutting one's shroud with one's own hands,
> Seeing one's death with one's own eyes!
> This death lies in ambush for thee
> Fear it, for that really is our death!

So, in this metaphysical vein, he goes on elaborating his answer to the problem of mortality and immortality—to the problem of human destiny. Ingeniously, step by step, he rebuilds for our benefit the edifice of his philosophy of Egohood. The edifice is undoubtedly impressive and will be of permanent interest to those who are versed in the architectonics of thought. If it is constructed out of a fabric no more enduring than that of Prospero's vision, so are most philosophies. But what matters is not the system of the philosophy which he builds, or the answers that he gives to the questions that he poses, but the questions themselves. And if we must have an answer, he has already given one in the *Zabur*. This is far more modest, less heroic perhaps, but it is more convincing. And it is more convincing because it is not so involved in any metaphysical and theological disputation: it is human and humanistic:

> Although I know
> That the idea of a destination,
> Is my own invention,
> Yet it is necessary,
> For to become way-weary

> In the midst of a journey,
> Is unworthy of man's courage.

The ardent pilgrimage itself is the destination. There is no destiny beyond the effort to create a destiny. There may be 'other universes beyond the stars', yet for the lover the trials of love are themselves the reward of love. That is the answer of the *'Psalms of the East.'* It is, perhaps, the eternal question reformulated, but it suffices.

Those, however, who are not satisfied with an imaginative restatement of the problem and desire an answer in more definite terms can turn to Iqbal's *Reconstruction of Religious Thought in Islam*, published by the Oxford University Press in 1934. The book represents Iqbal's most sustained and considerable effort in prose, indeed, the only one which deserves to be taken seriously. It consists of a series of six lectures which he delivered at the Universities of Madras, Hyderabad, and Mysore in 1928. The purpose of these lectures is to reinterpret the history of Islamic thought in the light of modern knowledge, and by so doing, to 'reconstruct' and refashion it. As in all his later work, the revivalistic argument is implicit in the 'Reconstruction'. It would be too much to claim that this factor does not detract from the enduring value of the book. For it does. But not so much, it must be added at once, as to place it on the same level as the bulk of revivalistic literature—it is almost a national industry—which has appeared in India during the past hundred years. It remains a work of very serious intent, eminently readable (a rare virtue that), instructive and provocative. It may or may not succeed in its revivalistic aims, but it unquestionably succeeds in recreating for us the essential aspects of Islamic thought and culture as an historic phase of world thought; and it does so more convincingly and clearly than most interpretative works produced by contemporary Muslim thinkers.

The importance of this achievement cannot be exaggerated. For of all the various world-views of the classical and post-classical periods of human history, Islam is the one which, owing to a combination of adverse circumstances, has received less attention than it deserves. Iqbal's attempt at a reconstruction of the cultural and philosophical heritage of Islam represents a pioneering work which will come to be increasingly appreciated by students of this important chapter in the history of civilization, no matter what we think of his revivalistic bias. For modern thought and modern science owe an enormous debt to medieval Muslim thinkers and scientists; and this debt is bound to be more generally recognized as modern research discovers a more balanced perspective and frees itself of its parochial Western European complex. Not the least significant merit of Iqbal's interpretation is the lucidity of his style, its freedom from that exasperating verbalism which characterizes so much writing which in India passes for 'profound' speculation, its astonishing precision in exposition of difficult and complex ideas.

The task which Iqbal sets himself in his *Reconstruction* is to vindicate the claims of the Qu'ran as the source and basis of a coherent, comprehensive and dynamic view of life. He starts by affirming that Islam, in its purest expression, has never accepted the duality between rational and positive knowledge and faith; that is, science, on the one hand, and intuitive, mystical experience, that is, religion, on the other. It regards the two points of view as representing a division of function, not a bifurcation of objectives:

> The truth is that religious and scientific processes, though involving different methods, are identical in their final aim. Both aim at reaching the most real... In the domain of Science we try to understand its [phenomenon's] meaning in reference to the external *behaviour* of reality; in the domain of religion we take it as representative of some kind of reality and try to discover its meanings in reference to the inner *nature* of reality. The scientific and the religious processes are in a sense parallel to each other. Both are really descriptions of the same world, with this difference only, that in the scientific process the ego's standpoint is necessarily exclusive, whereas in the religious process the ego integrates its competing tendencies and develops a single inclusive attitude resulting in a kind of transfiguration of its experiences.

He argues that 'the search for rational foundations in Islam may be regarded as having begun with the Prophet himself'. This argument inevitably leads to the suggestion, which he had already put forward in the *Asrar*, that all that is passive, fatalistic, obscurantist and other-worldly in Islam represents an excrescence due to the influence of Classical Greek thought. It was this influence, he maintains, which, though it broadened the outlook of early Muslim thinkers, 'obscured their vision of the Qu'ran... They read the Qu'ran in the light of Greek thought. It took them two hundred years to perceive—though not quite clearly—that the spirit of the Qu'ran was essentially anti-classical, and the result of this perception was a kind of intellectual revolt...' The revolt found its expression, he says, in Ghazali's philosophical scepticism whose mission 'was almost apostolic'.

He goes on to develop his conception of the spirit of Muslim culture. This spirit is not only anti-classical, and therefore modern, but takes its stand on the axiom that 'knowledge must begin with the concrete'. Iqbal quotes with approval the words of Abdul Quddas Gangoh, a Muslim saint: 'Muhammad of Arabia ascended the highest Heaven and returned. I swear by God that if I had reached that point I should never have returned.' This, he asserts, gives the clearest indication of the difference between the prophetic and the mystic types of consciousness:

> The mystic does not wish to return from the repose of unitary experience; and even when he does return, as he must, his return does not mean much for the mankind at large. The prophet's return is creative. He returns to insert himself into the sweep of time with a view to control the forces of history, and thereby to create a fresh world of ideals. For the mystic the repose of 'unitary experience' is something final; for the prophet it is the awakening within him of world-shaking psychological forces, calculated completely to transform the human world. Thus his return amounts to a kind of pragmatic test of the value of his religious experience...

And it is on this prophetic example that the Muslim culture has always developed during its most creative phases. All lines of Muslim thought, according to Iqbal, converge on a dynamic conception of the universe—a view which 'is further reinforced by Ibn-i-Maskwaih's theory of life as an evolutionary movement, and Ibn-i-Khaldun's view of history'. The structure of Islam, therefore, is not and has never been static: it is conceived in terms of 'the principle of Movement'. Iqbal sums up his interpretation of Islam in these words:

> As a cultural movement Islam rejects the old static view of the universe, and reaches a dynamic view. As an emotional system of unification it recognizes the worth of the individual and as such, rejects blood relationship as a basis of human unity. The search for a purely psychological foundation of human unity becomes possible only with the perception that all human life is spiritual in its origin. Such a perception is creative of fresh loyalties without any ceremonial to keep them alive, and makes it possible for man to emancipate himself from the earth. Christianity which had originally appeared as a monastic order was tried by Constantine as a system of unification. Its failure to work as such a system drove the Emperor Julian to return to old gods of Rome on which he attempted to put philosophical interpretation.

Islam, Iqbal maintains, not only freed the human mind from the static view of the universe, it also liberated it from the Magian and Messianic complex—indeed, from the burden of prophecy. This is the meaning of the concept of 'the finality of prophethood' which the Qu'ran teaches. No more prophets after the Prophet—that is the message. Henceforth man is to create his own new ideals by perfecting and developing his ego, his personality. He is to make his own destiny through his own exertions. That is precisely the meaning of *ijtihad*, which means 'to exert', and which represents 'the principle of movement in the structure of Islam'.

Iqbal then surveys the working out of this principle in the contemporary world of Islam and comes to the conclusion that 'the claim of the present generation of Muslim liberals to reinterpret the foundational legal principles, in the light of their own experience and the altered conditions of modern life, is, in my opinion, perfectly justified. The teaching of the Qu'ran that life is a process of progressive creation necessitates that each generation, guided but unhampered by the work of its predecessors, should be permitted to solve its own problems.'

What are these problems and how are they to be solved? Iqbal returns to his Kingdom of God on earth. 'Humanity needs three things today,' he asserts, 'a spiritual interpretation of the universe, spiritual emancipation of the individual, and basic principles of a universal import directing the evolution of human society on a spiritual basis.' And only Islam, rid of its excrescences and impurities, can provide these three things. For with the Muslim 'the spiritual basis of life is a matter of conviction for which even the least enlightened man among us can easily lay down his life; and in view of the basic idea of Islam that there can be no further revelation binding on man, we ought to be spiritually one of the most enlightened peoples on earth. Early Muslims emerging out of the spiritual slavery of pre-Islamic Asia were not in a position to realize the true significance of this basic idea. Let the Muslim of today appreciate his position, reconstruct his social life in the light of ultimate principles, and evolve, out of the hitherto partially revealed purpose of Islam, that spiritual democracy which is the ultimate aim of Islam.'

The exhortation is interesting as are the arguments which Iqbal uses to prove his case. These arguments will convince the convinced; and the exhortation will move the faithful, if not to action, at least to admiration. But that is not the point. The point of the *Reconstruction*, apart from its attempt to place the development of Islamic thought in a new, more intelligible perspective, is in the argument which is never stated but which is there all the time behind his words and behind his arguments, insistent and inescapable, providing the unconscious but compulsive motive of the whole work. It is essentially the argument of the Aligarh Movement restated in more coherent terms. In Iqbal that movement has, as it were, come of age; and the *Reconstruction* is the witness of its maturity.

For the underlying theme of this work is the need, not only of the rediscovery of the past of Islam, but its rationalization in order to bring its ideals into line with the practical contigencies of the age and the world in which Iqbal lived. The rediscovery of the past of Islam itself is necessary only with a view to providing it with a rationale in terms of the present. It is significant that Iqbal uses the phrase 'pragmatic test' even in relation to the Prophetic revelation. In spite of his revivalistic bias, he is really anxious to find scientific sanctions for Islam, trying to adjust its values to the values of modern times. This is precisely what the Hindu reformers from Raja Rammohan Roy to Tagore had been trying to do with Hinduism. The stream of Muslim Renaissance in India thus runs parallel once again to the current of Hindu Renaissance—but with a time lag.

There are, of course, differences of detail, of form; but these are relatively unimportant. What is important is the identity of aim and purpose. For Iqbal, though outwardly opposed to the ideas of liberalism, ranges himself on the side of liberals who want to refashion the 'foundational legal principles' of Islam, which means nothing more nor less than their adjustment to the actuality of the new social relations. He wants reforms, though not revolution which might destroy the 'spiritual values' of Islam. He wants the modern generation 'to solve its own problems' guided, but not hampered, by orthodoxy. He wants change, in other words, within the framework of the existing social order, change without tears. He is accepting all the bourgeois virtues and values, a little surreptitiously perhaps, but accepting them wholeheartedly. For an avowed anti-liberal, Iqbal has stated the doctrine of Islamic liberalism remarkably well in his *Reconstruction*. A Luther in the world of Islam, after all, is not such an impossible phenomenon.


The six lectures which form the content of *Reconstruction of Religious Thought in Islam* were delivered in 1928. During 1931-2 Iqbal had the opportunity of visiting Europe in connection with the Round Table Conference. He made use of this opportunity to travel through France, Italy, Spain, and on his way back, Egypt. It was his visit to Spain that he found most stimulating. For the journey was a kind of *recherche du temps perdu*. He was not visiting the Spain of Alcala Zamora, but of several centuries earlier—Spain which had witnessed the flashing sword of Tarik. Nostalgically, he was living through the Islamic past of the country. He visited Cordova to see that magnificent monument of Islamic architecture—the Mosque of Cordova. After the expulsion of the Arabs from Spain, as is well known, the Church Militant had the heart of the mosque converted into a cathedral by means of certain constructional alterations, including the pulling down of sixty-three of its original 1200 columns and the building of a *Crucero*, or high altar and Cruciform choir, in the interior—an act of vandalism which brought forth from the Christian king Charles V the gentle rebuke: 'You have built what could be built anywhere and have destroyed what could be found nowhere else on earth.'

For Iqbal's nostalgic vision, however, these constructional changes were as though they were not. Behind and beyond the cathedral he saw the mosque; and behind and beyond the mosque the glory and greatness that was Muslim Spain. He was moved; and when he was moved he always wrote movingly. The poem which he wrote while sitting in the Mosque of Cordova was published in his collection of Urdu verse, *Bal-i-Jibreel* (The Wing of Gabriel), and it contains some exquisitely lyrical lines:

> Hidden in your dust are the marks of ardent
>                                            prostrations.
> Your morning breeze carries within it the silent call
>                                        of the Muezzin to prayers.
> Your beauties need once more the carmine touch of
>                                                      *henna*,
> For there is still colour left in my life-blood.
> I have seen; I have shown; and I have heard; and I
>                                       have made others listen to me.
> Yet the heart's consolation is not in seeing and not in
>                                                           knowing.

This journey through time and space was important and fruitful, but even more important and fruitful was the journey on which Iqbal was engaged during these crucial years—a journey which took him beyond space and time. The itinerary of one's physical self does not always coincide with the itinerary of one's spirit. For the spirit of man has its own wanderlust and its own journeys to make to satisfy that wanderlust. While Iqbal was touring through western Europe and the Near East, even while he was attending the dull and melancholy sessions of the Indian Round Table Conference at St James' Palace, his mind was completing a voyage through all the planetary heavens and the nether regions.

He had long wanted to make this voyage. He had made great preparations for it ever since he wrote to his friend in 1903 of his immortal longings. It is not quite certain when exactly he embarked on this strange adventure, though from internal evidence one would be justified in suggesting that it was not begun till after 1930, at least not begun in earnest. But there is no manner of doubt that it was completed by 1932 when his *Jawid Nama* was published. The book, in Persian, is apparently named after his younger son, Jawid. But the word *Jawid* has a dual significance. For it literally means eternal. A true rendering of the title in English would, therefore, be the 'Book of Eternity': for 'Eternity', indeed, is the subject-matter of this long cycle of poems.

There is some reason to believe that Iqbal looked upon *Jawid Nama*, if not as his *magnum opus*, certainly as one of his major works. And it is a major work: it is the book 'in the manner of Milton's *Paradise Lost*' which he had once desired to write. At least, it is the nearest he got to fulfilling his wish. Milton, perhaps, is not a good parallel. It would be more accurate to refer to Dante. That reference, however, raises controversy. Many Muslim admirers of Iqbal are very touchy about any suggestion that Iqbal borrowed any ideas from outside the orbit of Islam, or even to the suggestion that he borrowed any ideas at all. They claim that Iqbal was inspired to write *Jawid Nama* by an idea which is as old as the Qu'ran—the idea of *Miraj*, or ascension of the Prophet to the presence of God; and though they admit that Iqbal could not have claimed the privilege of ascension which was reserved only for the Prophet, they maintain that Iqbal was following the tradition of Muslim mystics in describing his vision of heaven and the other regions.

But these arguments are silly and only reveal the imbecile level to which literary criticism has been reduced in India during the present age of unreason. There can be no doubt that Iqbal was aware of the parallel of *Divina Comedia* while writing his 'Book of Eternity', even though he was aware of other purely Muslim parallels. After all, if Iqbal derived any inspiration from the great Florentine while tracing out his other-worldly itinerary, he was only returning a compliment. The poet of Christianity had derived considerable stimulus, while planning his voyage, from Muslim travellers who had preceded him on the same route. As Professor Asin Palacios has observed, Dante owed no small debt to the ideas of Ibnu-l-Arabi. 'The infernal regions,' he writes, 'the astronomical heavens, the circles of the mystic rose, the choirs of angels around the focus of divine light, the three circles symbolizing the Trinity—all are described by Dante exactly as Ibnu-l-Arabi described them.' And Professor Nicholson, who quotes Professor

Palacios in his chapter on Islamic mysticism in the *Legacy of Islam*, goes even further:

> Dante tells us how, as he mounted higher and higher in Paradise, his love was made stronger and his spiritual vision more intense by seeing Beatrice grow more and more beautiful. The same idea occurs in a poem of Ibnu-l-Arabi written about a century earlier (*Tarjumanu-l-Ashwaq*, No. LV):

Meeting with Him (the Beloved) creates in me what
                              I have never imagined...
For I behold a form whose beauty, as often as we
                      meet, grows in splendour and majesty,
So that there is no escape from a love that
                increases in proportion to every increase in His
                loveliness according to a predestined scale.

The parallelism, general if not particular, is unmistakable. There are, of course, differences of detail in the pattern that is projected; differences, too, in the handling of the theme. The flora and fauna of the regions to which Iqbal takes us is not the same as described by Dante. For the two poets had different terms of reference; the Muslim eschatology obviously differs in important respects from the Christian. On the whole, it can be claimed, Iqbal reserves a somewhat milder destiny after death for those of whom he morally disapproves than Dante who was nothing if not fierce and passionate in judgement. But this may well be because Iqbal is far more interested in his visit to those regions where the saints and martyrs dwell than the lower depths to which the votaries of the fallen seraphim are relegated for their sins. While Dante devotes the greater and perhaps the most significant part of the *Comedia*, to the description of the Inferno, Iqbal never takes us to what could be called Hell, properly speaking, though he does take us to the abode of those whom even Hell has rejected.

There are also other differences. Dante had a guide in Virgil and a goal in Beatrice. In *Jawid Nama*, Iqbal finds his guide in Rumi, but there is no Beatrice—or, if there is, we are not allowed to witness the goal. Once again strict purdah is observed; and as far as we can judge, the journey itself is the end of the journey. There is a difference of scale. The 'Book of Eternity', though by no means a minor work, is not conceived in the same dimensions as the

*Comedia*. This reduction of the scale of the landscape may again well be due to Iqbal's preoccupation with the quality of goodness or near-goodness and his comparative unconcern regarding the quality of evil which occupies so large an area of Dante's mental universe.

Despite these differences, however, there is a fundamental identity of imaginative purpose. Both Dante and Iqbal have attempted to re-evaluate the significant historical experience in terms of their respective world-views. But for Dante the task was relatively easier. He lived in a world where there was as yet no serious challenge to Christianity, its doctrines and its values. After the *Summa Theologica* of Aquinas, after the *Tresor* of Master Brunetto, with the Church at the height of its power and the concept and reality of Christendom largely intact, a Christian poet had only to create his world to be believed. But Iqbal had to do his revaluation in a more trying and sceptical age; he had to apply Islamic values to historical experience while knowing that his readers were conversant with Marx and Freud; and he had to try to re-establish the validity of Islamic ideals at a time when Kemal had kicked the last relics of the second Caliphate into the dust-bin of history and when Bokhara and Samarkand, where once the Crescent had flown, had linked their destiny to the Red Star.

It was demonstrably an impossible task. But, then, Iqbal was always undertaking impossible tasks. Like Rumi's seeker who sought 'what could not be found', Iqbal, too, was always seeking the absent, the unattainable. He suffered from what psychologists might describe as *soif de l'impossible*. *Jawid Nama* does not succeed in carrying conviction and in that sense it fails in its essential purpose. But the failure, like all Iqbal's failures, has its moments of majesty and magnificence of utterance.

It is permissible briefly to trace the course of his voyage through Eternity. At the beginning of the poem we find the poet lost in a monologue with himself. It is the twilight hour and the scene arranges itself on the edge of a river. 'Though thirsty and far from the source of the spring' the protagonist involuntarily begins to sing a famous poem by Rumi. This serves the purpose of a spiritual invocation. Tearing apart the veils which hide the immortals from the mortal eye, Rumi's spirit appears before Iqbal in all its splendour.

Immediately a long dialogue begins. Iqbal's role is that of a prompter with certain leading metaphysical questions. Rumi answers—at length. The main discourse revolves round the nature of life and the meaning of *Miraj*—the Ascension of the Prophet. Life, Rumi declares, is a process of 'assimilation, intoxication, burning (with desire) and aching'. Ascension, he adds, signifies a revolution in the very centre of one's awareness. The poet is stirred to the very depths of his being by Rumi's 'instruction'. This is not surprising since Rumi is merely putting into eloquent verse Iqbal's own *Weltanschauung*.

At this stage, however, there is an interruption. The Spirit of Time and Space appears on the scene to take both Rumi and Iqbal on their celestial voyage. The first port of call on the route is the lunar heaven. Here the travellers encounter an Indian mystic on their arrival. He lives in a deep cavern under the Moon's surface and is, presumably, meant to typify the ascetic and the world-renouncing kind of consciousness. Paradoxically, however, Iqbal gives him the name of 'the Friend of the World', the implication being that asceticism and renunciation are only a subtler form of bondage to the world of matter. The Friend of the World puts forward his world-view which consists largely of a mixture of sophistry and self-hypnotising verbalism:

> The Universe is from attributes,
> And Truth is without attributes.
> What then is the Universe?
> What is man?
> And what is Truth?

Rumi has a very sharp answer to this riddle, 'Man,' he says 'is the Sword, Truth is the one who wields the Sword, and the Universe is the stone on which the Sword is sharpened.' He goes on to put forward the thesis that 'the East has seen the Truth, but not the Universe and the West has been preoccupied with the World and has moved away from the Truth.' This by no means original or historically correct aphorism impresses the Friend of the World; and he now begins to put a whole series of questions which have evidently been troubling him in his cavernous retreat. Rumi answers them briefly, for both he and the poet are pressed for time. The dialogue ends somewhat inconclusively.

The pilgrim and his guide now start on a tour of what the Higher Beings call 'the Valley of Testaments'. It is the realm of prophecy, the valley of vision. The first testament is that of Gautama Buddha. It takes the form of his sermon to a courtesan which leads to her conversion.[1] It is one of the most moving passages in the 'Book of Eternity'; and it is witness to the regard which Iqbal entertained for the world-renouncer of Kapilavastu, notwithstanding the latter's philosophy of complete renunciation of desire. The second testament is that of Zarathustra who is shown here as being tried by Ahriman. Zarathustra sums up his view of life by saying: 'Life is the revelation of oneself.' The third testament is that of Jesus, interpreted by Tolstoy. The last testament is the testament of the Prophet of Islam which we hear through the lament of the soul of Abu Jahal in the precincts of Ka'ba. Needless to say that it is the last testament which represents for the pilgrim and his guide the way and the life: for it forms the basis of a religion 'which cuts the ties of country and race... and in the eyes of which the high and the low are one'.

From the lunar heaven we move on to Mercury. Here we encounter two important personages, Saiyed Jamal-u-Din Afghani and Saiyed Halim Pasha, two Muslims who were Iqbal's precursors in many ways and preached the doctrine of Pan-Islamic unity. The visit gives Iqbal an opportunity for propounding his political and social philosophy through the lips of these immortals. The discourse ranges over the various concepts of polity such as religion and nationality, socialism and capitalism, the Caliphate of man, Divine Government and the idea of the general good. Afghani ends by sending a message to the Soviets in which he advises them to turn to the Qu'ran and not *Das Kapital* for their socialist polity. Why? Because the Qu'ran, he declares, contains the death warrant of the master and upholds the rights of the disinherited of the world, the workers, *des bons sans-culottes*.

There is a brief call at the heaven of Venus where there is an assembly of the gods of the ancient world. But the shore leave is, as it were, very short and the pilgrim and his guide have time only to hear a song of Baal which has the refrain:

---

[1] See Chapter XII.

O ancient gods, time is time.[1]

There are also one or two other encounters, including one with Pharoah. But very little of interest is said and the world of Venus is as dull as the Assyrian Room in the British Museum.

The next heaven, that of Mars, is much more stimulating. For it is the habitat, in so far as they have any habitat, of those who in their constitution and spiritual make-up are the complete opposites of the earth-dwellers. For while the earth-dwellers are prisoners of their physical bodies and have their 'heart bound in water and clay', it is just the reverse with the inhabitants of Mars—here the body is the bondsman of the heart. It is not, however, the inhabitants of Mars who are so interesting: it is the world in which they live, and especially Marghdin the metropolis of Mars which we are shown, that is the chief point of interest. For in this world, as the wise man of Mars tells us,

> There is no one who is a beggar,
> No one who suffers privations,
> No prayers and no priests,
> No ruler and no subject.

It is, in brief, a completely Utopian universe where there is no frustration, no failure, no despair.

But the pilgrim must move on. He belongs to the world of the living and he has no time to linger—even in this other-worldly Utopia. We follow him to the planet Jupiter. Here we meet those spirits who, though of the Kingdom, have yet somehow missed the Kingdom. They were not taken into paradise, though they truly belong to it. So they have become the eternal wanderers, the celestial vagrants. But saints *manqués*, in the very nature of things, are more entertaining than saints proper and in Mercury we encounter two spirits of the highest eminence. There is the Indian poet Ghalib and there is the Arab mystic Hallaj who cried *Ana'l Haqq* (I am the Truth) and was executed in Bagdad in AD 922 for this and many other divine presumptions. It was Hallaj who, when brought to be crucified, uttered these memorable words:

> And these Thy servants who are gathered to slay me, in
> zeal for Thy religion and in desire to win Thy favour,

---

[1] The phrase Iqbal uses is ambiguous. My friend the late Dr Nazir Ahmed Shah interpreted the phrase as meaning: it's time to start. I must abide by his interpretation.

forgive them, O Lord, and have mercy upon them; for verily if Thou hadst revealed to them what Thou has revealed to me, they would not have done what they have done; and if Thou hadst hidden from me what Thou hast hidden from them, I should not have suffered this tribulation. Glory unto Thee in whatsoever Thou doest, and glory unto Thee in whatsoever Thou willest!

For a soul of such order, heaven or no heaven, there cannot be any question of repentance, since it can create its own heaven. Hallaj speaks in the 'Book of Eternity' in the same inspired and memorable language which he had used when facing the cross. This is how he defines his conception of heaven:

> The Heaven of the priest
> is conceived in terms of slaves and *huris*;
> The Heaven of those who are free in the spirit
> Is eternal wandering.
> The Heaven of the priest
> is eating, dreaming and music;
> The Heaven of the Lover
> is the spectacle of the Beloved.

And he goes on to indicate the quality of his love:

> My love is stranger to all complaints
> Although it knows tears of ecstacy.

And his advice to the pilgrim is 'to renounce speech and hearing and to allow himself to be submerged in the being.'

Ghalib is less eloquent. But, perhaps, that is an unfair way of putting it. It would be truer to suggest that he has the eloquence of reticence, of silence. For he knows the difficulty, one might almost say, the impossibility, of trying to utter the unutterable. And, in any case, it is now time for yet another and undoubtedly the strangest of encounters. This is with no less a person than the first of the truants from God, the fallen seraphim, Satan himself. No poet and mystic has been able to make a celestial voyage without at some stage coming across this remarkable soul. Iqbal is no exception. His conception of Satan is that of the archetype of those who have, out of an infinite and insatiable passion for God, deprived themselves of His presence. He is called 'the master of the tribe of those who are destined to suffer permanent separation from the beloved'. His nature is a stranger to the taste of the union with the beloved; his way is the way of the denial of eternal beauty. But there is a magnificence about him—the magnificence of a courage that is beyond despair. For only one possessed of such courage could say:

> The order of life is from the ache of absence.
> O, blessed ecstacy beyond ecstacy of the day of
>                                                 separation!
> My lips can never utter the word of union,
> For if I were to desire union
> Neither the beloved would remain nor I.

And his heart's cry ends with the words:

> It is, perhaps, rapture which I find in defeat.

The appearance of Satan is possibly an indication that we are within sight of the other place. But we are never granted vision of Hell proper. We only visit the region of *Zahal* or Saturn which is meant for those whom even Hell has rejected. It is, therefore, important to know who they are. Iqbal describes them as the lowest and meanest of souls; and it is significant that he should include in this category those who have betrayed their people and their country—all the quislings of the world. It is an intimation of the value he placed on freedom—at least in theory, if not in practice.

No sooner have we crossed the ocean of blood than, we find ourselves confronted with the unhappy spirit of India. But she is not there because of her own sins, but because of the sins of some of her ungrateful and disloyal children. Iqbal describes her in words which are at once tender and exalted, as though he had rediscovered something of his early patriotic fervour. As she draws the veil from her face, she reveals

> A brow in which shines eternal light
> And in her eyes eternal rapture.

With all these graces, however, bondage is her melancholy destiny and on her lips are heart-rending cries. Why? Because, she laments, Indians are strangers to the honour of India. And she goes on to complain:

> How can my night end in the day's dawning?

Jafar is dead, but his spirit lives on to this day.

The last verse refers to the betrayal by Mir Jafar of Bengal to the foreigner—an act of treachery which opened the road to the British conquest of India. In Mir Jafar Iqbal evidently sees the prototype and symbol of all traitors and quislings; and it is not without significance that he reserves for this category the worst of all torments after death. Even Hell has excluded them. For the dwellers in Hell God is still a reality—even if as an everlasting absence. But for the traitor and the quisling even that saving grace is not there. His is, indeed, the worst of all damnations. For, as one of them rises from his Ocean of Blood to lament:

> This world is without a beginning and without end.
> For where is the God of the traitor?

The celestial voyage is, however, drawing to its close. There is only one more heaven to be visited. It is very populous and houses a very mixed crowd. Here we meet philosophers like Nietzsche for whom

> There is no Gabriel, no paradise, no *huri*, no God,
> But only a handful of dust burning with eternal longing.

There are poets like Ghani of Kashmir and Bhartrihari. The pilgrim asks the latter:

> Tell me from whence poetry derives its fire?
> Tell me, is it from the Ego or from God?

And Bhartrihari answers:

> The delight of my being is in the seeking.
> The fire of poetry derives from desire.

There are saints like Saiyed Ali Hamadani and eastern potentates like Nadir Shah Abdali, and Tipu Sultan. The latter emerges as the symbol of patriotic martyrdom. He asks the poet, who had recently visited southern India, how conditions are in that part of India and gives him a message to be delivered to the river Cauvery which flows by his palace at Seringapatam in Mysore.

It is now time for the pilgrim to depart from Paradise. The huris try to persuade him to linger a little longer, but he refuses.

The true wayfarer, he argues, is one who knows the urge of the journey and who fears the fascination of staying at the destination even more than the highway man. Yet something has so far been missing in all these encounters, something immensely important. For a celestial voyage without a vision of the beloved is Hamlet without the Prince of Denmark; it is so much wasted spiritual effort. Iqbal could hardly return from his planetary trip without a glimpse of the One who is the destination of destinations.

He is not disappointed in his purpose. We are treated first to a long poem on the meaning of His presence. Then we witness the Beloved—not directly, for that would be unbearable but indirectly. There is a dialogue between what may be described as the Divine Beauty and the poet. This is in the nature of preparation for the ultimate moment of apocalypse, of transfiguration. It could only be a moment, since eternity itself is not a horizontal extension but a verticle ascent, an instantaneous realization and revelation. As that moment comes, the light from the face of the Beloved tears open all the veils which have created illusions and mysteries. But the moment of unveiling is also a moment of silence—beyond all utterance. Like Moses before him, the poet loses his power of speech.

Not altogether, however. For he recovers it sufficiently on his return to earth to be able to address a message to his son Jawid, who is for him the symbol of the new generation. But this is only a restatement of what he had already summed up at the beginning of the 'Book of Eternity' through Rumi's lips:

> Art thou in the stage of 'life', 'death', or 'death-in-life'?
> Invoke the aid of three witnesses to verify thy 'Station'.
> The first witness is thine own consciousness—
> See thyself, then, with thine own light.
> The second witness is the consciousness of another ego—
> See thyself, then, with the light of an ego other than thee.
> The third witness is the consciousness of God—
> See thyself, then, with God's light.
> If thou standest unshaken in front of this light,
> Consider thyself as living and eternal as He!

> That man alone is real who dares—
> Dares to see God face to face!
> What is 'Ascension'? Only a search for witness
> Who may finally confirm thy reality—
> A witness whose confirmation alone makes thee eternal.
>
> No one can stand unshaken in His Presence;
> And he who can, verily, he is pure gold.
> Art thou a mere particle of dust?
> Tighten the knot of thy ego;
> And hold fast to the core of thy being!
> How glorious it is to burnish one's ego,
> To test its lustre in the presence of the Sun!
> Re-chisel, then, thine ancient frame;
> And build up a new being.
> Only such a being is a real being;
> Or else thy ego is a mere ring of smoke!

It is the building up of such a 'new being' of pure gold that he recommends in his admonition to the younger generation of Islam in the person of his son Jawid:

> O Son, learn from me the taste of vision,
> Learn from me burning in the intuition of God's unity.

And he returns to this theme later in the poem:

> Religion is to burn oneself completely in the search,
> Its beginning is in respect, its end is love.

Whether the younger generation of Islam, from the shores of the Mediterranean to the southern seas, have heeded or will heed his admonitions remains highly problematical. They may respond to other calls and worship other gods. As for those who do not belong to 'the peoples of the Book', the exhortations of the 'Book of Eternity' will be provocative but never convincing. But it is not for a philosophy or a way of life that one needs to go to Iqbal's poetry. Rather it is for that 'wealth by the wayside' of which he had spoken in his poetic preface of the *Zabur*. Of that incidental but none the less tempting wealth there is an abundance in *Jawid Nama*. There are lines of purest gold such as the following:

Life creates
From the delight of (the Beloved's) absence,
And presence
The image of this universe
Of proximity and distance.

It is not necessary to be a Muslim, it is not necessary even to be a mystic of any description, to find here the verification of the reality of an experience by no means alien to the spirit of man. Professor Ibrahim Poure Daoud, who visited India as a member of the Iranian Cultural Mission early in 1944, when asked his opinion about Iqbal, expressed the view that 'Iqbal was only a local poet'. Literary and aesthetic standards naturally vary from age to age and from country to country. The Iranians are welcome to their more 'universal' contemporaries. For India the 'local' poets are enough, since in this case the locality with which we are concerned is the limitless universe of the human heart itself.

Iqbal was prodigal with the 'wealth' found by the wayside. He literally lavishes it on his readers in his next book of verse—*Bal-i-Jibreel* (Wing of Gabriel). It appeared in 1935 and represents his last considerable poetic effort. For, though two more collections of his verse—*Zarb-i-Kaleem* (The Stroke of the Rod of Moses) and *Armughan-i-Hejaz* (The Gift of Hejaz)—were to follow, the last one posthumously, in these later works the lyrical and imaginative impulse is distinctly on the decline, the language is obscure, the expression tends to be verbose and even clumsy, and there is a general opaqueness which points to the involution of the spirit, the desiccation of the springs of inspiration.

No such defects, however, mar the *Wing of Gabriel.* In it the imagination can still soar, the flow of poetry is for the most part as easy and felicitous as in the *Zabur.* In fact *Bal-i-Jibreel* stands in the same relation to his Urdu verse as does *Zabur-i-Ajam* to his Persian verse. It is a work of maturity. The mood is, perhaps, instinct with an overtone of despondency, of frustration and loneliness. This note is struck at the very beginning in the two lines, adapted from Bhartrihari, which form the foreword:

> It is possible to cut the heart of a diamond
> With the petal of a flower.
> But upon the ignorant man
> Tender and delicate utterance is lost.

Iqbal, obviously, was by now despairing of ever finding an understanding audience. His solitude and frustration were, in a sense, self-inflicted, but he could still turn these into exquisitely tender and delicate poetry, capable of piercing hearts harder than a diamond. There is for instance the lyric in which occur the following lines:

> There are other universes beyond the stars;
> There are still other trials of love.
> Be not content with the world of colour and form,
> For there are other gardens and other nests.
> You are an eagle, flight is your nature,
> There are yet other skies stretching before you.
> Do not get entangled in this web of night and day;
> For you there are still other times and other places.

For Iqbal, however, there were no further poetic summits. The *Wing of Gabriel* is the last of the range which began with the *Asrar*, or *Secrets of Self*. After it the descent begins.

CHAPTER X

# The Lost Melody

The descent which began on the imaginative plane is paralleled on the physical. The latter, indeed, began somewhat earlier. From 1931 onwards Iqbal's health progressively declined. But before giving a chronicle of the last few years of his life, it is of interest to note another unusual feature of his career. For a man whose mind ranged over so vast a universe of thought and feeling, and whose imagination moved across the spacious planetary heavens, actual life revolved in a singularly narrow and constricted orbit. It is surprisingly devoid of the sense of spaciousness and freedom of movement. When he first came to Lahore he lived in one of the most congested localities of the city known as Bhati Gate. Later he shifted to Anarkali, a noisy and then fashionable shopping centre, where Iqbal lived for about ten years. When he became a little more prosperous, he moved to an unimpressive bungalow-style residence outside the city on a road with a Caledonian name—Macleod Road. His house was one among the many which were springing up in this suburb favoured by the professional middle class—lawyers, doctors, insurance agents; and if there was anything to distinguish it from the others, it was its relatively dilapidated frontage. Later this road was to become famous, not for the fact that one of the most significant poets of Asia was living in the neighbourhood, but because of several cinema houses which were built there in the years between two wars and which attracted large crowds of Lahore citizens every evening. Iqbal lived the major part of his life in the house on Macleod Road, but about three years before his death he had a house built for himself, and named Jawid Manzal after his younger son, in a less noisy locality on a road, which, to this day,[1] is named not after the

---

[1] This was true in 1956 when I revisited Lahore.

poet and philosopher of Pakistan, but a long-forgotten and undistinguished British Proconsul, Lord Mayo—Mayo Road.

Thus in Lahore his movements were restricted to an area of a few square miles. Nor was he a great traveller. True, he went to Europe for studies in his youth and visited England and the Continent. The Round Table Conference afforded him yet another opportunity for foreign travel; and this time he included the Iberian peninsula, Egypt and Palestine in his itinerary. He also made a journey to Afghanistan on the invitation of the Afghan Government (as a member of the three-man commission on educational reforms, the other two being Sir Ross Masood and Suleman Nadvi); and in the course of this trip he visited Ghazni among other places. Even inside India he did not travel much. Apart from his lecture tour in southern India, it is doubtful if he ever undertook journeys just to see places and discover India for himself. He was really only familiar with the Punjab, Kashmir and the North-West Frontier Province. He was never able even to realize an ambition which all good Muslims, rich or poor, cherish—the pilgrimage to Mecca. He had always wanted to visit the land of his heart's desire—Hejaz—but unfortunately left it too late; and then his health would not permit him to undertake the journey.

Compared to the wanderlust from which Tagore so fortunately suffered, and which took him to the ends of the earth, Iqbal was of a stay-at-home and unadventurous disposition. Partly because of this he never acquired an international reputation which can only come from having international contacts. But, then, it should be added, Iqbal was temperamentally reticent and reserved. He had quite exceptional gifts for friendship and had a very large circle of friends, but he had no flair for publicity which in modern times has become almost an attribute of greatness. He seldom sought the limelight and was not so fortunate as to find powerful champions of his work abroad as, for instance, Tagore did in Yeats.

His circumstances, moreover, did not permit him to indulge in the luxury of foreign travel. Though he never knew poverty, he was never affluent. Most of his life he had to manage on a very moderate income and budget his expenditure with some care to keep within his means. He had many rich Muslim admirers, but few of them carried their admiration to the practical level of helping him in the material sphere. And after 1931, when he gave up his legal practice owing to failing health, there are reasons to believe that he had some financial embarrassments. For though his books sold better than those of most Indian poets, it is not possible for anyone to live by poetry or on poetry alone—least of all in India where the reading public which can afford to buy books is very small and the habit of buying books is *rara avis* among those who can afford to buy them. It was only the generosity of the Nawab of Bhopal, who settled on Iqbal a pension of Rs 500 per month in 1935, which enabled him to spend the last few years of his life in comparative freedom from financial worries.

The fact, however, that Iqbal was not able to travel a great deal and visit foreign countries, and that he neither sought nor received world recognition, was in one sense fortunate. It saved him from the temptations to insincerity, to playing up to the gallery, and to resorting to the false coinage of glittering platitudes to please an uncomprehending public, which are the inevitable concomitants of fame and which even the best of men have found it impossible to resist. Iqbal's work is not without flaws, but it can be claimed with some confidence that it rarely descends into insincere and theatrical posturings.

His life was simple: his needs few; and there was very little of outward show about him. His house had no ostentatious furnishings; no streamlined limousines, which have become the hallmark of *nouveaux riches* respectability in India, ever waited outside his door. There was an atmosphere of easy-going informality around him; and he was immensely accessible. Anybody who wanted to see him did not have to fix an appointment; he had only to walk in. In summer he sat on a bed in the compound of his house, leaning against a bolster and wearing what may be described as a male *négligé*, Punjabi style, which meant a long shirt and *lungi*. Around his bed there would be chairs for the visitors. During the cold season the same order of things was observed indoors. And beside his bed there was always the inevitable *hookah*.

Iqbal was in the best sense of the word a popular poet. His poetry was read not only in select circles and among literary coteries, but by people who could claim no literary accomplishments. It was recited and sung by the roadside. I must record an instance illustrative of the extraordinary popularity which Iqbal as a poet enjoyed. While travelling from Mysore to Bombay several years ago by the less popular metre-gauge route which hugs the ghats, I heard somebody singing in a wayside station in the very heart of Kanarese speaking country. But the song was not in Kanarese. It was in Urdu. Through the still and warm evening air it traced a delicate arabesque of melody, and as it turned out, it was a poem by Iqbal which begins thus:

> O long-awaited Reality do reveal yourself
> In the garb of appearances,
> For a thousand prostrations are trembling,
> In my brow of supplication.

In spite of his great popularity, however, he never became what might be called an 'institution'. He preserved his humanity which is not always easy for celebrities. People came to see him from far and near: all sorts of people and they came for all sorts of reasons. Some came only to shine in the reflected glory of his greatness; others with more serious intent. But his doors were not barred against anyone. His was, indeed, the house with the open door.

His company was always exhilarating. On this point the evidence is unanimous. He was a brilliant conversationalist, but what is even rarer, and particularly with those who are good conversationalists, a good listener. The conversation in his company would range over every subject under the sun—from the awful 'searching sublimity' of Vedanta to the latest joke. He spoke for the most part in Punjabi, with occasional excursions into English, but rarely in Urdu—unless visitors from the United Provinces or Delhi happened to be present. His talk was never self-consciously brilliant though it was often profound; it was easy, suggestive but never assertive and it was always relieved by an inexhaustible and vibrant sense of humour. It is a misfortune that those who had the privilege of his company have been too lazy to record his conversations in a systematic manner. He could have done with a Boswell or an Eckermann. As it is, the world will have very little knowledge of this aspect of his genius.

The recurrent theme of his conversations, of course, was Islam and its future. On this subject he felt passionately and could be sentimental. It is said that he could seldom read or hear the Qu'ran being read to him without being moved to tears. The piety which he had learnt from his father apparently remained with him to the end of his days and even became more pronounced as he grew older. He was a believer not only in the spirit of the Qu'ranic word, but also the form and the letter. He observed all the austerities and was never lax in saying his prayers. The 'way of love' was not the way of licence or laxity for him.

In his early years he had tasted the pleasures of social life, but that was a very brief and passing phase. In his later years he did not go out much and, in any case, modern entertainments, like cinema and theatre, had no interest for him. He was definitely anti-modern in this as in many other things and his actual mode of life corresponded more to the patrician–feudal pattern than the contemporary bourgeois pattern. It had the old-world liberality and grace as well as its narrowness, uneventfulness, and monotony of cadence. Apart from talking to those who came daily to see him—and they were many—his chief preoccupation was reading. He was a voracious, but highly discriminating and selective reader.

For a man whose poetic output is certainly not slender, consisting as it does of nine full-size works in verse, it is surprising to find that he wrote at infrequent intervals and that there were long periods when he did not write at all. But when the mood of creation came to him the flow of poetry was copious. He always had a notebook and pencil beside him on a table so that, if the inspiration came to him, he could write down the verses or dictate them to anyone who happened to be present at the time. He wrote in a very clear hand; and his writing possesses all the decorative refinement of Urdu calligraphy, tending to terminal flourishes which, however, are never too demonstrative and, in fact, seem to fall naturally into line with the neat parallel lines of the text.

In his youth Iqbal was a familiar figure at the local poetic symposiums. During the years of his maturity he did not give so many public recitations of his poetry as in his youth, but he appeared at most public functions associated with the work of the Anjuman-i-Himayat-Islam, and at its annual session made it a custom to read a new poem. On a number of occasions he read his poetry to vast congregations of twenty to thirty thousand people after the prayers in the King's Mosque, Lahore. He had an attractive voice and moved his audiences as much by the content of his verse as by the melody of his voice. Towards the end of his life, however, he gave up the habit of public recital. The last recorded occasion on which he recited his poetry—it was his poem written during his visit to the mosque at Cordova—was at Jamia Millia, Delhi, in 1933.

His taste in dress was simple, and though most of the published photographs show him dressed in an European style of slightly archaic Edwardian flavour, he really preferred the Punjabi style dress with its quality of comfort and looseness. He never wore a hat except, possibly, during his early visit to Europe as a student. In later years his favourite headgear was the fez.

Like most Muslims of his generation, and indeed Muslims in general to this day, he was a liberal and generous host. He ate well, though only one main meal in the day. Pilau, meat cooked with or without vegetables, and *seekh kabab* constituted the normal and most favoured menu. As far as is known, he strictly observed the Islamic injunction regarding abstinence from alcohol. The only wines he ever tasted in his maturity, and tasted in an abundant measure, were the wines of imaginative ecstacy. And these were intoxicating enough. For the rest, his favourite beverage appears to have been tea, taken with a little salt and without milk, a preference which he probably owed to his Kashmiri inheritance.

Physically, he was an impressive presence, though less because of any remarkable physical feature and more on account of his lively personality. He was definitely not photogenic and most of his photographs do him less than justice, except one in which he resembles Nietzsche in profile—a fortuitous resemblance no doubt, but interesting to note in that he had many spiritual affinities with the German ecstatic. He was of a medium height and fairer in complexion than the average Punjabi—a characteristic which again must be attributed to his Kashmiri origin. He had thin, well-chiselled lips. But the most striking features of his face were the elevated and broad brow and luminous eyes indrawn in the tormenting flight of thought. He wore a moustache, but departed sufficiently from Muslim orthodoxy as not to keep a beard, the length of a man's fist, which the faithful are enjoined to cultivate.

This physical heresy, if one may so call it, once in his life, at least, deprived him of the blessings of a Muslim divine. It happened towards the end of his life. He had heard of a Muslim sage, Sher Mohammed, living in Sharakpur—a village not far from

Lahore—who had earned great reputation for his spiritual gifts through a life of great piety, austerity and in conformity with the Good Law. Iqbal went to see the saintly personality. Mian Sher Mohammed, when he saw the stranger, asked him the purpose of his visit. Iqbal explained that he had come to ask his blessings and to beg him to pray for him.

Sher Mohammed was a man of very high spiritual attainments, but high spiritual attainments are not always enough to liberate one from certain obsessions about matters of form. He had an obsession about beards and firmly believed that it was easier for a camel to pass through the eye of a needle than for an unbearded Muslim to enter the Kingdom of Heaven. He advised everybody who came to him for guidance and advice to cultivate a beard—regulation length. He told Iqbal point-blank that he could not intercede with God on his behalf since he had shaved off his beard.

Iqbal got up and walked back to the cab-stand which was some distance from the village. Meanwhile someone had recognized Iqbal and told Sher Mohammed who the stranger was whom he had turned away so unceremoniously. The poor unsophisticated divine was greatly upset at what he had done. He ran after Iqbal and managed to catch up with him just as the latter was getting into a *tonga*. He apologized profusely for his rudeness and explained that his admonition regarding the keeping of a beard was meant only for the ordinary Muslims. For one whose services to the community were of such outstanding order, he added, there was no need to worry about such minor observances.

A certain tragic maladjustment is inherent in the natural order of human existence. For, generally speaking, afflictions and sorrow come to man not when he is best equipped to endure them, that is, in his youth, but in his old age when he no longer has any strong mental or physical defences left and when his power of resilience is at its lowest ebb. The last few years of Iqbal's life were even more than normally unhappy. First, there was the pang of an intimate estrangement. He had cut off all relations with his eldest son. The story of this estrangement is a subject of considerable psychological interest which is told briefly in the last chapter. For our purpose it is enough to explain that Iqbal entertained patriarchal notions regarding the duties and respect which a son owes to his father. In his own childhood the father-figure had been the most important and idealized symbol of authority; and he expected from his own sons the same degree of obedience and filial devotion which he had shown towards his father. These expectations were too high; and it is not surprising that his eldest son revolted against his father's authority. Iqbal in turn literally cut him out of his life—and, of course, his will. He tried to compensate himself for this intimate tragedy by concentrating all his affection on the younger son Jawid Iqbal and his daughter Munira Begum. But compensation, in the very nature of things, is compensation: it approximates but never becomes the equivalent of the thing itself. And there is little doubt that the void created by this estrangement remained and rankled like yet another thorn in the spirit.

In 1935 another blow came, the death of his second wife. This bereavement at a time when his own health was fast deteriorating heightened his premonition of death and he knew that he had not long to live. It was a year before the death of his wife that he had developed an affliction of the throat which led to local paralysis of the laryngeal nerves, resulting in partial loss of voice. It is related that he developed this affection after eating a kind of vermicelli in hot milk on the *I'd* day in 1934. He must have neglected the infection, and his throat got progressively worse. What is more, even when he began to take his illness seriously, he was very unsystematic and even irrational in the treatment which he chose, alternating between the modern and the ancient, the allopathic and the Greek system popular among Muslims. He went to Bhopal, for instance, to have electrical treatment for his throat, but later abandoned this for indigenous, empirical cures.

Besides the paralysis of the laryngeal nerves, he had long suffered from kidney trouble. Treatment had mitigated but never wholly cured it. Periodically, it recurred and brought in its train inflammation of the lower limbs. With years the attacks became more frequent and more acute. In 1937 yet another affliction fell upon him. He developed cataract in his eyes and his vision was affected.

This was hardly calculated to add to the sum of his happiness. First the voice had gone and now the sight was going. One by one life was taking away what it had given. The physical certitudes were falling away, vanishing. Soon the heart was affected—not the heart which he had described as 'my ocean, my boat, and my shore as well'—but the suction-pump which lies between the ribs. He suffered from acute palpitations and found it difficult even to walk a few steps to go to the bathroom. And there were other ailments—asthma, for example—to complicate matters and add to his winter of discontent. Treatment continued, erratic and variable as ever; first the doctors, then the indigenous medicine-men—among the latter, two well-known *Hakims*, the famous Hakim Nabeena (so named because of his blindness) of Delhi and Hakim Mohammed Hussain, principal of the Lahore College of Greek Medicine—tried their skill. But in vain. His strength was steadily declining.

The human body is an inadequate, pathetic, at times even humiliating instrument for heroism and heroic philosophies. In so far as it is possible for the human spirit to transcend the limitations of its physical frame, Iqbal's spirit during this period of illness transcended them. There was a certain quality of equanimity, of serenity which remained with him despite all his afflictions. In between fits of asthma he talked as exhilaratingly as ever to his visitors. Indeed, if sometimes his friends remained silent for fear of making him strain his throat in trying to talk to them, he would insist that they should talk because, he said, 'he felt better when talking'. His one main pleasure, reading the Qu'ran alone, he could no longer indulge in; instead, however, he had it read to him. His one major anxiety, even in these days of acute physical suffering, was still his fears about the future of the world of Islam. He was not optimistic and confessed to grim and melancholy forebodings; sometimes there were even tears.

But beyond pleasure, beyond anxiety, beyond forebodings and tears, there was a sense of security, at least, about his personal destiny. He had no anxieties on this count: his faith had done that much for him, if no more. One day when his elder brother, seeing his suffering, began to weep, Iqbal comforted him with these words: 'Why are you crying? Is it because you are worried about my death? But death is not something to weep over. I am a Muslim and I am not afraid of death.' An essay in spiritual Couéism no doubt, but it worked, at any rate, for him.

Outside, the brief north Indian spring was moving to its end and the long travail of the heat and drought of the early summer months was almost upon the earth. Iqbal's life, too, was rapidly drawing to its close. By the middle of April, as the nights were already getting warm, his condition had become worse. He brought out blood as he coughed and his heart was getting weaker. On the evening of 20 April, the doctors told his friends and relatives that the end was a matter of a few hours. Iqbal himself knew it to be so, but showed no symptoms of distress or agitation. He had, as it were, made his peace with death long ago. A friend who was with him on the night previous to his death has recorded this episode:

> The poet asked Diwan Ali to sing to him a Punjabi song. The poet's request served as a happy interlude. It proved that the poet was still extremely alive mentally, even four hours before death. Diwan Ali sang a few verses of the mystic poet of the Punjab, Bulleh Shah. These verses seemed to touch a very tender chord in the poet's heart, and tears trickled down his cheeks...

But these were tears of ecstacy rather than of despondency. It is related that the same night he dictated the following quatrain which was meant to be his epitaph:

> The lost melody may or may not return,
> The gentle breeze may or may not blow once again
>                                                           from Hejaz,
> Another wise man may or may not be born,
> But the days of this *faqir* are done.

The first part of the night he had slept moderately comfortably. About three in the morning, however, he awoke and became restless. Restlessness increased and soon after five o'clock he touched his heart and murmured: 'God, how it aches here.' His old and faithful servant Ali Bakhash who was beside his bed held his head in his arms to comfort him. And in a few moments the melody which had stirred so many people, and for such diverse reasons, was, indeed, lost. Such was the end.

# CHAPTER XI

## To Sum Up

The end, however, was also the beginning—of canonization, if not apotheosis. As the news of Iqbal's death spread through the city, crowds began to gather outside his house, Jawid Manzil. They included every strata of the population of Lahore, rich as well as poor, literate no less than illiterate. All the local notabilities were, of course, there to pay their last homage; even those who had neglected him during his lifetime were in at the funeral. Courts, schools and colleges were closed in his memory. A vast procession of some forty to fifty thousand people followed the body to the burial place in the shadow of the King's Mosque—the very mosque from which on rare occasions he had recited his verse to enormous congregations and moved the hearts and minds of men. But now the voice was silent and beyond the edge of the grave no one could follow him.

Yet for a man like Iqbal a new kind of life begins at the moment of death. Millions of words were spoken and written to the glory and greatness of the departed. Newspaper encomiums, commemorative poems, reminiscences, critical essays in literary journals were published. Full-length studies of his work, his philosophy, his personality followed in due course. Moreover, as the movement of Muslim separatism gathered momentum in the decade following his death, the stream of literature about Iqbal swelled into a flood. He became the prophet and the symbol of new political loyalties. Writing on or about him became a national industry of the Muslim intelligentsia, just as today in India writing about Gandhi has become a national industry. His greatness, which needed no magnification, was magnified out of proportion and out of focus. He was praised uncritically and, therefore, made to look somewhat unconvincing, even a trifle ridiculous. The process continues to this day and is likely to continue and become even accentuated so long as the present mood lasts. For new nations need heroes; more even than heroes they need philosophic sanctions. And for Pakistan there is nobody else, Qaidi-i-Azam Jinnah not excepting, who could fit the rôle of a national philosopher but Iqbal.

All that has happened and will happen to Iqbal is intelligible. But it does not solve the problem of those who want an objective understanding. For objectivity is one thing and hagiography quite another. Even the dead, D.H. Lawrence has written somewhere, only ask for justice. Especially the dead, perhaps, because they cannot defend themselves either against their detractors or their over-zealous admirers. This renders it incumbent upon one, even in a tentative sketch of Iqbal's life and work such as the present, to attempt some sort of a summing up.

But how is one to sum up a multi-dimensional personality like that of Iqbal; a personality so rich, so complex, so full of glaring contradictions? To every summing up there must always be something to add. A variety of interpretations are possible; they are even necessary. With a man whose writings are so provocative, so assertive, so dogmatic even, there is bound to be a wide margin of controversy in the assessment of the worth of his work.

There are, obviously, two broadly demarcated, though interrelated, aspects of his personality. There is the poet; and there is the prophet of Indo-Muslim renaissance. These two aspects may, and perhaps should be, considered separately. As a poet his reputation is based on far less controversial grounds than his reputation as a prophet of Pan-Islamic ideas. For his achievement in the sphere of poetry is so monumental that no matter how much we subtract from it there still remains enough, and more than enough, to sustain his pre-eminent position among the Urdu and Persian poets of our time.

Yet here a striking paradox has to be noted. Notwithstanding this monumental achievement, Iqbal has exercised singularly little influence on the generation of poets who have followed him. Most of them have admired him for one reason or another; most of them have been willing to acknowledge his supremacy; but hardly anyone among them has followed in his footsteps and their work shows no direct and palpable traces of having been influenced by Iqbal. This is an astonishing contrast to the case of Tagore. For whereas Tagore became the literary glass of fashion and mould of form for a whole generation of Bengali writers, and not only Bengali writers, this cannot be claimed of Iqbal. He has left behind him no school of poetry to carry on his tradition. The younger Urdu poets, Muslim as well as non-Muslim, have been inclined to worship other outlandish poetic gods—not Iqbal.

Possibly the explanation for this paradox is furnished by the fact that he was never preoccupied with formal and technical problems as such. He never experimented with new techniques and new forms in verse. He was not, in form and technique, fond of innovations. He broke no new ground in so far as poetic media are concerned. He was perfectly happy working within the framework of conventional patterns and rhythms. Though he had been influenced by the European Romantics and was temperamentally akin to them in many respects, he adhered to orthodox and traditional modes of poetry. The younger generation of Urdu poets, on the other hand, have been in revolt against these traditional moulds and forms. They have primarily been concerned with breaking away from orthodox patterns and conventions and only incidentally with discovering new content. They can, therefore, derive little direct stimulus from Iqbal.

Iqbal used the conventional patterns of Urdu and Persian poetry; he employed the well-established rhyming schemes and cadences; he remained for the most part faithful to the old symbols, metaphors, similes, imagery and allusions. But it would be a mistake to conclude from this that his poetry is merely a variation on old themes and breaks no new ground. For this is not the case. The surprising as well as the important quality of his poetry is that, though remaining strictly within conventional limits of form, it communicates an urgent and undeniable sense of originality. More than that: it succeeds in vastly expanding the scope and limits of existing forms, in making these forms infinitely more elastic and comprehensive than they had been in the hands of his predecessors. The old metaphors and similes in his hands acquire not only wider but a different kind of meaning; the traditional imagery and symbolism become completely transformed and carry new significations and fresh nuances in his usage; and allusions which superficially are derivative of the classical Persian poetry on closer scrutiny reveal themselves as being instinct with a deeper suggestiveness which can directly be related to contemporary awareness and experience. It is, indeed, a case of new wine in old bottles and there is great substance in the claim which Dr M.D. Taseer makes in his introduction to *Aspects of Iqbal* that Iqbal's verse 'is not topical but contemporary'.

It is in precisely this highly individual use of existing poetic forms and materials that Iqbal was original. He took these forms and materials and lifted them to a higher level, translating them to a new imaginative purpose. Before him Urdu and Persian poetry had largely been either purely descriptive, or purely technical in the sense of reducing itself to verbal virtuosity, or an expression of moods in the language of lyricism. True, there had been Hali and some of his less successful disciples. Hali had redeemed Urdu poetry from the morass of subjectivity and personal expressionism, revived it, and restored to it some of its higher functions such as criticism of social and cultural values, expression of a point of view, and preoccupation with living problems. But it was left to Iqbal to take poetry right into the arena of life and to revitalize it to a point where it could adequately perform these higher functions. With him poetry became a true critique of life; it took upon itself the task of moulding social outlook—of 'ordering human responses and impulses', if we prefer the scientific language of Dr Richards; it became able-bodied and adult enough to affirm a world-view. Whether that world-view was valid or not, whether the kind of ordering of our responses and impulses which Iqbal desired was in fact in conformity with the present needs, and whether his critique of life was correct or false—these are separate questions which are not germane to our argument at this stage of the discussion. What is germane is that he, more than any recent poet in India, was responsible for making poetry an effective vehicle by re-establishing its organic connection with social and historic processes. That is his distinctive contribution as a poet.

And it is a very great contribution. For in a sense he had a sharper and deeper appreciation of the functions of poetry than some of the experimentalists and innovators who came after him. He never succumbed, philosophically at any rate, to the lure of the ivory tower. He rejected vehemently the dogma of 'Art for Art's sake'. In his little note on 'Our Prophet's criticism of contemporary Arabian poetry' he declares: 'There should be no opium-eating in Art. The Dogma of Art for the sake of Art is a clever invention of decadence to cheat us out of life and power.'

Thus far, it will be observed, he was entirely on the side of the angels, not *fin de siècle* aestheticism with its doctrine of social irresponsibility of the artist. But, of course, he chose his own special angels on whose side he wanted to be; and his choice is not likely to be universally approved because it is a highly individualistic choice. He brought to poetry a modern approach as well as a vast new content of ideas which it had hitherto lacked; he handled contemporary themes as few before him had dared to handle them. But at this point his modernity ends; a regressive tendency begins to assert itself; and an unresolved duality becomes manifest. For, though he dealt with modern problems and themes in his verse, his interpretations are not necessarily in conformity with the contemporary spirit. There are reasons to believe that he was not unaware of this divergency in himself. True, he could boast that he had 'no need of the ear of today' since he was 'the voice of the poet of tomorrow'. But he also admitted in one of his poems his essential difficulty:

> I see tomorrow in the mirror of yester night.

This would be even truer if we substitute the word today for tomorrow. He saw the present in the mirror of yesterday. This divergency between the reality and the image is at once the principle of development in relation to his imaginative problems and the reason for the baffling translucency of his vision. It is the principle of development in the sense that there is in Iqbal the ever-present and insistent urge to eliminate the divergency, to make the image conform to the objective reality: and it is the cause of the translucency in his vision in that, because of his upbringing, his position in the society of his time, his inhibitions and complexes, he was unable to take the one step which would have solved the problem—namely changing the mirror.

Had he done so, however, it is also possible that he might have ceased to write poetry as has sometimes happened. For poetry is in the quarrel, in the tension and contradiction of an imaginative conflict. That is, at least, the case with Iqbal. He belongs to two different worlds, of today and of yesterday. His poetry is of both: it forms a kind of bridge between the past and the present. Across that bridge others will pass, if they have not already passed, wholly into the present—one hopes into the future, too. But that passage was not for him. That is the nature of a bridge, whether it bridges a gulf of space or of time: it forms a link, but it is not the road. Iqbal is the link. Standing on the edge of two epochs, it can be claimed, he represents the last in the chain of classical poets of the Indo-Persian order and the first of the Moderns. That is his significance.

The perspective is not so clear when we come to treat of him in his prophetic rôle and consider the social, political, and philosophical ideas which he propagated or with which he has become identified. It is not so clear because it is impossible to trace through his work any coherent, systematic and lucid schema of arguments on any of these planes. What we get, instead, is a turbid eclecticism, often brilliant and provocative, but which, in the very nature of things, could never acquire consistency of texture. His was not, despite many claims to that effect, a synthesizing intellect. Like most social, political and cultural eminences of India during the past hundred years, from Raja Rammohan Roy through Sir Saiyad Ahmed Khan to Gandhi, his mental background consisted of a mixture of all kinds of ideas; and this mixture constantly approaches a quality of synthesis but never quite achieves it. The pattern of thought that is projected is not, consequently, an integral whole, but a mosaic of variegated elements, though certain elements are more accentuated than others. And this is so, once again, because the essential dichotomy is the same in the case of the prophet as it is in the case of the poet. For as a prophet, too, Iqbal stands between two epochs, the old feudal and patriarchal and the modern capitalist–bourgeois. He belongs partially to both and wholly to neither, sharing the excellences no less than the defects, the illusions no less than the certitudes of both.

In such a personality there is bound to be confusion; and there is confusion. But there is also more than confusion. There is an aberration of vision, an ambivalence of thought and act. It is hardly surprising that there should be inconsistencies in his outlook; that there should be a divergence between what he preached and what he practised, between what he consciously set out to achieve and what he achieved or was instrumental in achieving. These inconsistencies and divergencies derive from that historic dichotomy which we have already noted.

In the political and social sphere, he aimed at creating what may be called an extra-territorial, supra-national loyalty based on the identity of ideals rather than one dependent on the accident of birth, race, colour, or social status. But in reality he succeeded only in stimulating the growth of a very virulent species of nationalism among his community—a nationalism which demanded a territorial focus as the condition of its appeasement. It is no good for the late Edward Thompson or others to quote Iqbal's private assurances that he believed Pakistan 'would be disastrous to the British Government, disastrous to the Hindu community, disastrous to the Muslim community' in face of the fact that he openly demanded the centralization of the living body of Indian Islam in a specific territory—and this after abjuring territorial loyalties.

Iqbal was in his social and political philosophy an anti-secularist, though he would have repudiated that label by vehemently maintaining that Islam recognized no duality between the secular and the spiritual, between the Kingdom of God and that of Caesar. But that is begging the question. Paradoxically, however, the fact remains that the sum total of his political and social influence has been to provide the necessary impetus of ideas, philosophical sanctions, the rationale indeed, to an essentially secular political movement, originating in the economic ambitions and aspirations of a particular group though masquerading under denominational disguise and unfurling a religious banner. The ideal in its translation to the plane of the real has thus undergone an inversion. But that inversion cannot be merely explained away as due to the perversity of the translators or an accident of history: it has come about because it is inherent in the ideal itself. The nature of the seed can only be judged from the fruit.

The contradictions and the inconsistencies are manifest throughout the whole fabric of his social and political ideals. He was a bitter critic of the liberal democratic tradition of the West based on the equality of stomach as he claimed it to be. Yet he found it possible to participate in the mock democracy of the Montford Reforms, which did not go as far even as stomachs. He lamented that the soul of Mir Jafar, who had betrayed India to the foreigner, was still alive; yet he felt no qualm of conscience in accepting the knighthood of the Empire which the Mir Jafars of India had been instrumental in bringing into being. He raised his voice in loud protest against the inequities and injustices of a society based on capitalist values. Yet he became the president of an organization which included some of the biggest capitalists of his community and was prepared to do political deals on the basis of percentages, division of spoils, demarcation of spheres of influence. More than that: the ardent critic of imperialism was prepared to assure the British Empire that the Muslims of north-west India would be prepared, at a price, to become 'the defenders of India against a foreign invasion', be that one of ideas or bayonets (shades of Cold War twenty years before the event). These may all have been tactical moves, but his philosophy recognized no such duality of ends and means.

To stress these contradictions and inconsistencies is not to prepare the ground for an adverse judgment, nor even to suggest that he was doing something morally reprehensible. The moral question, in any case, is not under discussion. What is at question is the relation of theory to practice. In this case the practice that flowed from a theory which was couched in the most idealistic terms was no different to the practice of the liberal social reformers and politicians of his time and class. It represents merely the continuation and development of the Aligarh tradition.

Related to the question of his critique of existing social and political values is his attitude to socialism. Dr Taseer has claimed that Iqbal 'became avowedly a Muslim socialist'. And in support of his claim he has argued that while in the *Payam* he had placed Lenin no higher than Kaiser Wilhelm II, in *Bal-i-Jibril* he honours Lenin sufficiently to take him in the presence of the Heavenly Host. There is substance in this argument to the extent that during the last few years of his life Iqbal felt increasingly the impact and challenge of socialist ideas as nobody could fail to do in the present age. It is true also that he wrote a number of poems during this last phase which strike a deceptive revolutionary note. There is, for instance, the oft-quoted 'God's fiat to his Angels' in which God commands the angels:

Arise and awaken the disinherited of my earth,
Shake the dwellings of the rich to the very
                                                    foundations.
That field from which the peasant derives no
                                                    livelihood
Burn every ear of corn from that field.

Such sporadic emotional outbursts, however, cannot be taken seriously as socialism, or even as 'Muslim socialism', whatever that ambiguous term may imply. For the fact is, as W. Cantwell Smith in his brilliant book *Modern Islam in India* has rightly pointed out, 'he never knew what socialism is' though 'towards the end of his life some of his friends were able to convince him that he really did not understand socialism, and he was preparing to remedy this ignorance when he died'. One might add, speculative though such an assertion must be, that had he lived long enough to complete his study of socialism, he would have still rejected socialism because he would have found its basic assumptions to be destructive of the dogmas on which he built his airy structure of a theocratic charitable social order.

His critique of capitalist social relations, and the inequities and injustices arising from these relations, was essentially from the standpoint of a Utopian—but a very special kind of Utopian. For his Utopianism was not of the same order as that of the eighteenth and nineteenth-century thinkers like Rousseau, Saint-Simon and Fourier, which started from concrete analysis of society in terms of concrete urgencies and forces which create and destroy social patterns, even though this analysis did not go far enough and got mixed up with strong elements of wishful fantasy. His Utopianism was abstract, metaphysical, closer in spirit, if not in form, to the kind of Utopianism implicit in St Augustine's *De Civitate Dei*. It was rooted in his emotional and intellectual fixation on the idyllic relations of a pre-capitalist, feudal social order. To equate it with socialism, in any of its modern forms, is completely to misrepresent socialism and Iqbal's social philosophy.

The relation of Iqbal's ideas to Humanism is equally negative. Admittedly, there is a humanistic urge behind his attempt to reinterpret and reconstruct Islamic polity and ideals in an historical perspective, to claim for these a validity in terms of modern necessities, and to rationalize their dogmatic structure. But this urge is subconscious, involuntary. The avowed aim of his philosophy is to give a 'spiritual interpretation of the universe'. This, in other words, signifies that a purely human destiny and the making of man 'the measure of the universe' did not satisfy him. It is true that he asked man to raise and develop his ego to such a point that:

## To Sum Up 143

> Before every decision of fate
> God would ask of man
> Tell me: 'What's your consent.'

But this affirmation which is his closest approach to Humanism merely envisages the possibility of convergence of God's will and man's at some point and under exceptional circumstances. It does not equate the two, much less eliminate the former from the scheme of reality. It still recognizes God's will as the ultimate and transcendental arbiter of the human situation. A world-view based on such a premise must inevitably fall within the orbit of the metaphysical rather than humanistic philosophies of our time.

Finally, there remains the problem of Iqbal's ethical and spiritual ideals. It is in truth only another aspect of his philosophical position; and the self-division is even more manifest, more poignant on this level. It could not be otherwise. Iqbal's spiritual and intellectual development, as has been noted, falls into two distinct phases. The thought-pattern of the one is in some respects almost the complete antithesis of the other—at least in its overt signification. During the first phase the matrix of his thought was represented by Sufi mysticism, with its doctrine of Immanence, linked on the one side to Neo-Platonism and on the other to Vedantic Idealism. He felt strongly the fascination of the ecstacy of contemplation, the rapture of the individual self merging in the universal. During the second phase, however, he completely and even passionately repudiated this ideal. Instead he affirmed the perfection of 'the ego' or selfhood as the value of all values, the *summum bonum* of the life-process; and he went on to preach 'action' and 'desire' as the basic means of realizing that perfection. Rising in the still waters of quietist and contemplative philosophies, his thought ultimately reaches a doctrine of unlimited dynamism.

It is clear that a mind which traversed so abrupt a trajectory of thought and belief could not but create for itself almost impossible problems of readjustment and reorientation. The mental conflict, in fact, was never wholly resolved; and behind and beyond the conflict, as we have suggested, there were sharp pangs of doubt, uncertainty, and even regrets which account for the strange, Rilke-like elegaic note which runs through his later verse. With such a translucent spiritual and intellectual back-ground, it is inevitable that the ethical ideals at which he arrived should partake of that translucency. They oscillate between an ambivalent moral eclecticism and a self-hypnotic, didactic dogmatism. But that is not the whole point. The point is that ideals, in the last analysis, must be judged in terms, not just of their facial import and intentions, but of their actual results. The word, indeed, acquires its true character and reveals its real, inward nature only in the process of becoming flesh.

Iqbal's word in the process of becoming flesh reveals its paradoxical and contradictory nature in a startling measure; and it does so because these paradoxes and contradictions are inherent in its very nature. The exalted ethical and spiritual ideals preached so vehemently by the most idealistic thinker produced by modern Islam, on closer scrutiny, appears to be highly suitable for conversion to purely practical, materialistic ends. His philosophy of dynamism, his ideal of the 'Ego' or 'Self' which must be developed to the uttermost limits of its possibilities and beyond those limits, his doctrine of 'assimilation' or 'absorption', were precisely the intellectual and spiritual stimuli which his group and his class needed in its struggle for the advancement of its material ambitions and interests, for a better political and economic destiny. These were the psychological and moral ingredients of the new attitude, the new world-view which was essential if it was to pull itself out of the slough of despondent passivity and fatalism, to gain self-confidence, and to stir itself to activity in a deliriously active world where the devil took the hindmost. These ideals were the perfect equipment suited to the needs of a rising capitalist society anxious to make up for lost centuries of opportunity, to consolidate its base of operation, and to achieve the maximum of expansion in the minimum of time. In a very different way, and given the vast differences of historical context it could not but be a very different way, Iqbal's doctrine of individual perfection has had, and was bound to have, the same liberating influence on the Muslim mind as the individualistic doctrine of the thinkers of the Renaissance had on the Christian mind. For his perfect 'Ego', the superman of his conception, who can not only claim 'divine vice-regency' but even 'absorb' God into himself, may have Qu'ranic antecedents, but he is also of the contemporary world where we meet him as the busy, bustling entrepreneur, the pioneering capitalist, the enterprising captain of industry and finance, the master-builder of the modern bourgeois social order. The democracy of 'more or less unique individuals, presided over by the most unique individual possible' which is Iqbal's idea of the Kingdom of God on earth is but an idealized version of the existing order of things and it almost reminds one of some of the Wellsian fantasies about the ideal order of society. The last great metaphysical poet and philosopher of Islam was also, strange and sacrilegious though it may sound to some of his admirers, perhaps the first of the bourgeois ideologue of the Muslim world who is worth listening to.

At this point the connection between Iqbal's ideas and the movement of what is known as Indo-Muslim renaissance becomes demonstrable. It was not a fortuitous and incidental connection, but fundamental. And it is of great importance. Without him this movement would be a movement without a soul, certainly without self-consciousness. And the posthumous popularity leading to canonization which he enjoys among the Muslim intelligentsia becomes intelligible—inevitable. W. Cantwell Smith has explained Iqbal's remarkable influence among the Muslims of India in the following words:

> Almost everyone found something in him to applaud, something which stirred him to renewed Islamic vigour. There were those, of the liberal school, who read Iqbal, and were merely proud of him—were proud that modern Islam had produced so great a man. Others, however, were incited by Iqbal's message to some degree of activity in the name of their Lord. They could not but see that the world about, or within, them was less good than it might be; and the poet's eloquence stirred them to do something about it—and to co-ordinate their doing it, more or less precisely with their Islam. Islam as a religion has produced no intellectual modernization of its idea of righteousness more explicit than Iqbal's. He is great because he said with supreme eloquence, and convincing passion, what his fellows were beginning to

feel, but were unable to formulate. Any modern Muslim who would talk about religion must begin where Iqbal left off; otherwise he is not worth listening to.

This is an excellent and succinct summing up of the nature and reason of Iqbal's influence. But it needs qualification. In some directions it needs clearer specification; in others amplification. For instance, when it is said that everyone found in him something to applaud, it obviously means every Muslim intellectual and in general the middle class. For though Iqbal was a popular poet whose reputation went far beyond the educated classes, for the masses it could not but be a legendary reputation—as in fact most reputations during the past fifty years in India have been legendary. But to the Muslim middle class and to the Muslim intelligentsia he meant something very definite; he gave them a faith and a doctrine which corresponded to their objective and subjective needs. He objectified and articulated their aspirations and ambitions. He did more: he provided the necessary veneer of idealization and rationalization even for their confusions. He was able to do so because he himself shared these confusions; for it is impossible to win a popularity, as he has achieved posthumously, without striking a chord of emotional identity. That is why Iqbal's popularity will endure as long as the confusions of our age will endure.

What will come after? The answer is a truer appreciation of his personality and his work. When that comes it will probably be seen that notwithstanding his revivalism, notwithstanding even his profoundly religious outlook, he prepared the ground for his people to be able to transcend the very outlook which he so passionately wanted to revive. For he accelerated the transition of the Muslim mind from a feudal to the modern frame. As a prophet, no less than as a poet, he bridges the gulf between yesterday and today. And that gulf had of necessity to be bridged in order that there could be a tomorrow. That is the summing up of his contribution which is immense. But, in the nature of things, there will always be something to add.

CHAPTER XII

## Matters of No Importance?

Iqbal regarded the practical and private details of his life as of little or no importance. However, these days by common consent these things—such as our passions, affections, ambitions, even lusts and greeds—are considered the very stuff of most biographical writing. Iqbal is however on record as having advised his serious biographers to steer clear of them. In the Preface to *The Ardent Pilgrim*, when it was first published in 1951, I quoted his precise words in this context, and those can bear repetition. 'There is no necessity,' he said to his friends and would-be biographers, 'to record these trivial details. The most important thing is the exposition of my thought and the tracing of the mental conflict [I had] in the evolution of my thought.' By and large, I heeded Iqbal's admonition when I originally wrote this book, although some of the intimate details were not hard to guess. They were, therefore, hinted at rather than spelt out, primarily because there existed at the time only circumstantial evidence for them.

In the past four and a half decades, however, a great deal of material has been published about Iqbal, both in India and Pakistan, which claim him as their own across an unreal frontier; especially since 1977 which, for some unknown and arbitrary reason, was assumed to be the centenary of his birth, though all the evidence points to an earlier date. Much of this material trades in irrelevancies and tends to trivialize Iqbal as has been the fate of all our truly great men and women. Some of it has, undoubtedly, the ring of authenticity and unveils significant aspects of Iqbal's personality; it cannot be ignored in any biographical study, no matter how tentative, bearing as it does on his relations with men and women who entered his life at different stages.

Inevitably, it includes the three women, Karim Bibi, Sardar Begum, and Mukhtar Begum he married successively in 1893, 1910 and 1913; his two sons, Aftab and Jawid, born of his first and second wives respectively: two daughters Meraj (who died very young) and Munira Banu; and many other friends. It also reveals to us something of Fraulein Emma Wegenast who, though younger than Iqbal, was one of his teachers in Heidelberg and with whom he formed a special attachment which was more or less Platonic. There is, more-over, the diary and other writings of Begum Attia Faizi whom he first met in London, in 1907 and whom Rafiq Zakaria in his book on Iqbal describes as his 'heart-throb'. But Iqbal seems to have had other heart-throbs—the earliest of whom was Amir, a singer and dancer. Iqbal loved her to distraction in his early years in Lahore. She was to him, if not Beata Beatrice (née Portinari) to Dante, something approaching her.

The reasons for Iqbal's reticence over his intimate relations seem to lend themselves to various interpretations, high-minded and not so high-minded. In a larger and more profound sense, he was, of course, right. Poetry, like all true art, is a state of grace that transcends the personality of a poet or an artist. The proper study of a poet is his or her poetry and the inner tensions that created it. Nothing else matters in the least in the ultimate reckoning. While the private things in Iqbal's life could be duplicated in the lives of others—and in the milieu and the times in which he lived, they were fairly commonplace—what made his poetry uniquely compelling could not be easily paralleled. Yet, as Donne reminds us, no man (or woman either) is an island and we are what we are largely because of other lives that impinge upon or intersect ours. Hence the importance of relationships which we form in the determination of our human condition, positively or negatively— and perhaps, both.

Iqbal, half in jest, described himself in one of his couplets which has been quoted earlier, as the sum of contradictions. But many truths are often uttered in jest; and when he said that he was a sum of contradictions, he was making a true avowal about himself. His reticence regarding what he considered trivial details might well have been due to the vanity of the public figure that he had become. We expect of our public men and women the virtues of saints, particularly in the Indian context, where we live in one of the most imperfect and flawed of societies, knowing full well—to alter a little of what the great bard said about virginity—that it is not politic in the commonwealth of nature to find unalloyed virtue, and most saints have had their fall from grace at one time or another in their lives.

After all, Iqbal was a man of flesh and blood. He had all the weaknesses and failings of one, if anything in a heightened sense because of his antecedents over which he wished to draw a veil. That he was fully aware of it we know from Attiya Faizi whom he met while both of them were in London in 1907 and of whom he grew exceedingly fond: he wrote a poem, not a very good one, as a gift-offering to her. She reciprocated his sentiment and their friendship lasted a lifetime. He once told her that he was a man divided; there was an internal self and an external self in him. The two were at variance, one with the other, if not perpetually in conflict, thus vindicating Yeats' belief that all human beings cultivate a mask which is in all things at total variance with what they really are.

This probably explains many contradictory traits in Iqbal. It certainly explains why he often said one thing and did quite the opposite. We all do it. But the philosophy he preached did not allow for any divergence between the word and the deed. The inner self in him might have been the fountainhead of his poetry and thought. It could spin out the most idealistic of philosophies and present it in the most seductive poetic form that lulled disbelief. But the man of flesh and blood—what the French call *l'homme moyen sensuel*—was incapable of living up to it. He frequently made compromises and even at times prevaricated. He recited a poem in celebration of the Allied victory at a public meeting in 1918 at the behest of the Lt.-Governor of the Punjab—none other than Michael O'Dwyer—which is pure bathos. Yet the following year, he attended in December a joint session of the Muslim League and the Khilafat Conference, not the joint session of the Congress and the Muslim League with which it is sometimes confused, by, among others, the distinguished writer on Iqbal, Rafiq Zakaria. It is true that both were held at Amritsar because earlier that year—on 13 April to be precise—the city had witnessed General Dyer's exploits. But the annual session of the Congress was presided over by Motilal Nehru, while the President of the joint session of the Muslim League and the Khilafat Conference was the well-known Muslim nationalist leader, Hakim Ajmal Khan. It was the latter's audience that Iqbal treated to the recital of his poem *Asiri* (Slavery) to mark the release from internment of the Ali brothers during the

First World War years.

However, notwithstanding that, his attitude to British imperialism seems to have remained extremely ambivalent, as has been discussed elsewhere. He always hankered for some recognition from it in a tangible form and never abandoned hope of preferment except in the last few years of his life when he was too ill. As early as 1901, two years after passing his MA from Government College, Lahore, he appeared in the examination for entry into the Provincial Civil Service (the Punjab cadre). He was successful, but failed to make the grade because his eyesight did not meet the stipulated standard owing to weakness of his right eye. On hearing the news, it is said on good authority that he broke down and wept. Leading Muslim papers criticized the decision of the medical board and accused them of prejudice against Muslim candidates, which was probably the case. The British had not yet transferred their favours from the Hindus to the Muslims, although the time for it was fast approaching. It, however, never seemed to occur to the leader writers of Muslim papers that this could be a blessing in disguise. Iqbal was meant for higher things than the post of a Deputy Commissioner or a Sessions Judge of a district to swell the ranks of the British administration. Fortunately, that immense tragedy was averted by the 'prejudice' of the medical board.

With time, especially after his knighthood in 1923, he set his sights on higher things. He broke with Abdul Qadir because it was rumoured that Irwin (later Lord Halifax), when Viceroy and Governor-General of India, wanted to appoint Iqbal the Lt.-Governor of the North-West Frontier Province. He is supposed to have consulted Abdul Qadir and Fazl-i-Hussain, who was at the time a member of the Governor-General's Council. Both are said to have counselled Irwin against the move on the ground that the British establishment, which disapproved of polygamy, would be shocked at polygamous Iqbal, who had three wives (in point of fact, at the relevant time he had only two surviving wives, the third having died in 1924), becoming the Governor of the most critical province in India. The story is probably apocryphal, although Aftab Iqbal, Iqbal's elder son, believed it. The British intelligence in India and elsewhere kept a tab on everything in the private lives of all notable persons in their vast Empire, and some of the unnotable ones, too. It would have been consulted and it would surely have let Irwin know of Iqbal's plural matrimonial status before he consulted either Fazl-i-Hussain or Abdul Qadir.

Even if it were true that Abdul Qadir had intrigued with Fazl-i-Hussain to deprive Iqbal of a lucrative preferment, in a written interview which Arshizada had with Aftab Iqbal in April 1978 and which the *Sha'ir* published in its special issue devoted to Iqbal, Aftab revealed that Abdul Qadir sought Iqbal's forgiveness. According to Aftab, Iqbal told Qadir that he could forgive him but it would be hard to forget. However, Iqbal never really forgave or forgot Abdul Qadir's 'duplicity' any more than he forgave Aftab's sins, if sins they were. Yet Abdul Qadir had been Iqbal's friends from his days in London, and even before. Indeed, it was he who persuaded Iqbal not to give up his poetic vocation when Iqbal was seriously contemplating abandoning his muse for some more substantial—and no doubt more profitable—pursuit. As the editor of the *Makhzan*, a serious literary monthly in Urdu, Abdul Qadir published many of Iqbal's poems and other writings when Iqbal was less well-known.

With Fazl-i-Hussain his relations were more complex—and, perhaps, more bitter. Political differences of a fundamental nature entered into them, but it is scarcely possible to avoid the impression that envy was part of the psycho-pathology of that relationship. Fazl-i-Hussain, after a brief flirtation with the Congress, had changed sides and had taken a broadly 'loyalist' position. As a co-founder of the Unionist Party, which represented the interests of big and medium landowners—the squirearchy, in fact, in undivided Punjab, as already suggested—he was an eminently successful and effective politician. Indeed, it would not be far wrong to suggest that the Unionist Party in Punjab was the only secular party because the Congress politicians, with rare exceptions, were drawn from the urban middle class, largely Hindu, who fell in varying degrees under the influence of the Arya Samaj founded by Swamy Dayananda from Gujarat, who led the Counter-Reformation in Hinduism in the second half of the nineteenth century.

Certainly, Fazl-i-Hussain in his lifetime formed the best bulwark against the Punjab falling under the influence of the Muslim League—and Jinnah. Iqbal moved closer to Jinnah partly because of his antipathy to Fazl-i-Hussain. For he had no great admiration for Jinnah and had earlier joined the Muhammad Shafi faction of the Muslim League because he suspected Jinnah of surrendering to the Hindus over the Nehru Report. Needless to say, the suspicion was unwarranted. Iqbal's lifelong and faithful servant is on record that when Jinnah came to Lahore some time in 1936 or 1937, he called on Iqbal in the early afternoon. Ali Bakhash duly announced this to Iqbal who was sitting in an armchair and as usual smoking a hookah. He did not respond to his servant's announcement. About a quarter of an hour or twenty minutes later Ali Bakhash announced again that Jinnah was waiting and that there was a woman with him (evidently Jinnah's sister, Fatima Jinnah). Iqbal was left with no option but to call them in. Aftab, who happened to be there that day (this is hard to believe), has recounted that after the two men were silent for about fifteen minutes, Iqbal asked Jinnah: 'Mr Jinnah what brings you here today?' And Jinnah replied:

> Well, Sir Mohammad Iqbal, after thinking a great deal about the problem of division of India, I must fully agree with you that the creation of a Muslim State carved out of India, as you demanded in your presidential address at Allahabad in 1930, is the only solution not only of the political problem of the Indian Muslims, but also of India as a whole.

To that Iqbal responded, with some acerbity, and rather disingenuously: 'I have been telling you that for the last seven years; have you realized it now?' The meeting was not particularly cordial—at any rate, far less cordial than his meeting with Jawaharlal Nehru when he came to Lahore and Iqbal sent for him. As already related, it was 'a few months before his death' and Iqbal was 'in reminiscent mood', Nehru tells us in his *Discovery of India*. At least, there were no long and awkward pauses in which both men were at a loss to say something to one another, as Aftab, who apparently was there that afternoon when the meeting between Jinnah and Iqbal took place, has narrated. After one such long pause, Iqbal asked Jinnah what kind of help he needed. Jinnah wanted Iqbal to consolidate the Muslim League in Punjab where it was weak, thanks largely to the Unionist Party and the influence of Fazl-i-Hussain. Iqbal appears to have consented to Jinnah's request. At the same time, however, he cautioned Jinnah:

> I shall be delighted to do so, but I must tell you that I want the Muslim League to be a Muslim organization, not of the big Zamindars (landowners) and capitalists.

The only thing I can give you in this province is the poor masses.

This was another of Iqbal's cherished illusions: that he could deliver the poor Muslim masses of Punjab to Jinnah and the Muslim League by the magic of his words. That magic was real, but it knew no boundary of confession, caste, or creed. Incidentally, Aftab, in the interview he gave Arshizada shortly before his death, revealed another of the 'secrets' that went into the making of Pakistan: that Iqbal was indirectly responsible for Jinnah's return to India from London, where he was practising in the Privy Council and had his chambers in an upstairs office of the King's Bench Walk.

According to Aftab, there was a meeting between Winston Churchill and Jinnah. Evidently Churchill said to Jinnah:

Mr Jinnah, why are you wasting time here? Why don't you go to India? Go and make up with the poet (Iqbal), work for the creation of Pakistan, because we want Pakistan.

Aftab has it that when Jinnah learnt from Winston Churchill that the Tory Party was prepared to pronounce its benediction on the Pakistan idea, he made haste to return to India and assume the leadership of the Muslim League. How far this account of the meeting between Churchill and the Qaid-e-Azam corresponds to reality, and whether such a meeting took place at all and is not a figment of Aftab's imagination, is difficult to say at this distance in time. But Jinnah had a pretty shrewd understanding of British politics, especially as regards India and other imperial matters, and it is difficult to give credence to Aftab's version of it. At all events, Jinnah was well aware that Churchill did not carry any substantial section of the Conservative Party with him in the bitter campaign he was conducting, with the assistance of Beaverbrook and his mass-circulation newspaper empire, against Stanley Baldwin's policy of 'Constitutional Reforms' in India embodied in the Government of India Act (1935). Many of the Tory MPs might well have sympathized with Churchill's stern policy against any concession to even the timid section of opinion in India, but dared not come out in opposition to the official line on India for fear of the consequences.

It is, therefore, much more likely that for family reasons Aftab was motivated by the desire to magnify Iqbal's role in the creation of Pakistan as against Jinnah's and embroidered the story of Jinnah's meeting with Churchill. That would add a touch of pathos to the story, for Iqbal's relations with his elder son during his lifetime were extremely envenomed. As Iqbal has left no record of Aftab's sins other than that his son was ease-loving and fond of pleasure and play, not studies, one has to assume that Aftab was more sinned against than sinning. Indeed, Aftab desperately yearned to reinstate himself in his father's affection, but never succeeded. Iqbal never forgave him and, indeed, cut him out of his will and was generally unkind to him to the point of cruelty. How had Aftab transgressed against Iqbal to have earned his father's enduring displeasure? That lifts a veil from a painful chapter in family history, the way Iqbal treated his first wife, Karim Bibi, whom he married in 1893 when he was about seventeen according to officially accepted mythology, and around 20, if we are go by more authentic data and accept 1873 as the year of his birth.

Iqbal was then studying for his matriculation. Actually, the news he had passed the matriculation examination in the first division— and it was about the only examination he passed in the first division—came during the marriage. Karim Bibi's father belonged to the professional upper middle class and was serving as a civil surgeon in Gujarat, then a district town in undivided Punjab. On retirement, Dr Atta Muhammad was put in charge of the medical services of the petty princely state of Malerkotla. On the other hand, Iqbal's father, a tailor by profession in Sialkot, belonged to the lower middle class—the *petite-bourgeoisie*. Such marriages were uncommon even among the Muslim community although, theoretically, Islam claims to be an egalitarian faith. What made Dr Atta Muhammad—Iqbal's elder brother bore the same name as his father-in-law—give the hand of his daughter in marriage to a young man who was socially well below him and whose prospects were at best problematical? It appears that Maulvi Mir Hassan, Iqbal's teacher in Arabic, Persian and Urdu, had been the go-between in the marriage of Iqbal to Karim Bibi. He had evidently persuaded Dr Atta Muhammad to agree to the match by convincing him that Iqbal had quite exceptional gifts and was destined to go very far—a

## Matters of No Importance?

prophecy which was fulfilled in an ample measure, though not in terms of a bank balance.

In the event, it did not exactly prove a happy marriage. Iqbal had a daughter by his first wife, Miraj Begum, who was born in 1896, and a son, Aftab Iqbal, who was born two years later. Karim Bibi gave birth to another daughter in 1901, but the child died in infancy. Miraj Begum, too, died young—in 1914, the year Imam Bibi, Iqbal's mother, died. Iqbal wrote a moving—albeit in the conventional pathetic mode—elegy on the death of his mother, but not his daughter. His wife, Karim Bibi, never wholly satisfied him, but the fault was not hers. Everyone who knew her testifies to her kindly and gentle nature. But she was a homely woman, not one who could serve as an inspiration to a poet, much less one who set men's hearts ablaze. Iqbal wrote a letter to Attia Faizi—and the two were mutually attracted—in which he set down some of the reasons for his marital discontents.

This letter was however written when both of them were back in India, early in April 1909. Among other things, he tells Attia that he had refused the 'chair' of philosophy offered him at Aligarh College (founded by Sir Saiyed Ahmed Khan for the Muslim youth) and had resigned the 'chair' of history at Government College, Lahore, because he did not want entanglements of service. He was embroidering a little. There were no 'chairs' in those days in Colleges and he did not tell her that he had been appointed temporary part-time Professor of English Literature and Philosophy in Government College, Lahore. As regards avoiding entanglements in service, he had just then accepted the post of joint editor of the *Law Journal* published by the Law Journal Publishing House in the capital of Punjab, Lahore.

Again, he was being economical with truth when he says in his letter to Attia that at the time of his marriage he had written to his father that he had no right to arrange his marriage. There is no record of any such complaint before the marriage was solemnized. Nor would one expect this of him. He was seventeen when he was married, according to official mythology, and about twenty, according to more reliable calculations. At the time he was rather pleased with the adventure in which he was, moreover, the focus of much attention. It is not every humble tailor's son who gets married to a civil surgeon's daughter. The bitter complaint against his father for this early marriage was, obviously, an afterthought. In all probability, his father-in-law also helped Iqbal financially to complete his education in Lahore and later to go to Europe for higher studies, although the only debt of honour he acknowledges in his letter to Attia Faizi is the one he owed to Atta Muhammed, his elder brother.

He goes on to tell Attia that his only wish is to escape from India and she knows the reason why. All the same, he spells out his reason for her: he is no longer prepared to go on living with his wife, Karim Bibi, and thereby waste his life. Every human being, he says, has the right to happiness, and if society or nature denies him that right, then he would raise a standard of revolt against both. He boasts that he has enough fire in him to burn down every social convention and custom. But, perhaps realizing that he is not made of the stuff of rebellious spirits—and the disarming thing about Iqbal is that he knew his weaknesses and strength—he decides to opt for the softer way of fleeing this 'ill-starred country' or taking to drink which makes it easier to commit suicide. He did neither. At any rate, he adds, he can find no comfort in the dead and barren leaves of books, whether his own or others' is anybody's guess.

The letter is really a *cri de coeur*. He knew that Attia would understand. That is why he wanted to go to Bombay to see her. In the very next sentence, with more cunning than subtlety, he touches her nerve of jealousy. Two or three weeks ago, he tells Attia, he had a letter from 'your friend' and one of his teachers at Heidelberg, Emma Wegenast. 'I like the girl', he writes, gratuitously adding, 'she is so good and truthful'. Apparently, Emma never married, for all Iqbal's letters to her are addressed to 'Fraulein', meaning 'Miss'. She was in love with Iqbal and the love was reciprocated—at least as long as Iqbal was in Germany between 1907 and some time early in 1908. Propinquity, as Aldous Huxley would say, was essential for love for Iqbal. He talked of going to Heidelberg to see Emma before leaving Europe for India towards the beginning of July 1908, but never did.

Iqbal and Emma Wegenast kept up a desultory correspondence till the catastrophe of the First World War intervened to interrupt it. When the war ended, the correspondence was resumed. Iqbal's first post-war letter was written from Lahore on 10 October 1919. He expressed sympathy for Germany and said that it faced 'a time of trial'. Earlier, he had written a poem celebrating the Allied victory at the behest of the Lt.-Governor of the Punjab. He anxiously asked

Emma about her brothers, but he gives her no details of his own life during the war years. He had really come to believe that they were of no importance.

However, that was not the end of the affair. The pace of correspondence quickened somewhat when he visited London for the Second and Third Round Table Conferences between the autumn of 1931 and the end of 1932. He had toyed with the idea of revisiting Heidelberg just to see Emma Wegenast. Indeed, in one of his letters to her, written towards the end of December 1932 from Queen Anne's Mansions, St James's Park, he gave the precise time of the train by which he would be arriving. He wrote, 'I am leaving London on Friday, 30 December. According to my present programme I reach Heidelberg on 18 January 1933 at 10.23 p.m.' He even gave the name of the hotel where he would be staying and added: 'The only object of my stay in Heidelberg is meeting you after so many years. I am looking forward to meeting you with great pleasure.' It is not exactly the letter one would expect a lover to write to his beloved after a very long separation, 'but that might have been because he was uncertain of her reaction if he presumed too much.'

He, however, never reached Heidelberg on the appointed night. His next letter to Emma was written from Madrid, three days after he was supposed to have been in Heidelberg. It said, all too briefly, 'I returned to Madrid from the South of Spain today. Sorry it would be impossible to come to Heidelberg this time. I had to cancel all the tickets I purchased from London as I must catch the boat [Count Verdi] from Venice on the 10 February 1933. I may be coming to England again in April.' But he never went to England again. If he had not been in two minds, he would surely have explained why he had gone to southern Spain. It was, obviously, to see the magnificent mosque in Cordova—which the Church Militant, after the expulsion of the Arabs from Spain, had converted into a cathedral as has been mentioned earlier—and to be seen and having himself photographed saying *namaz* there. Anyhow, if he had been terribly keen to see Emma, there was time enough between 21 January and 10 February, when he sailed for India in a Lloyd Triestino boat, to make a detour via Heidelberg. It was not as if Heidelberg was thousands of miles away from Madrid—it was, actually, only a 36 hours' journey by train even before the dawn of high-speed travel and the Jet Age.

His reason for cancelling his visit to Heidelberg were perhaps more complex than he had indicated in his letter to Emma. In 1907-8, he was comparatively little known outside the Punjab. Now he was an eminent poet, one of the great poets in Asia if not the greatest, and a knight to boot. He had still a lingering ambition, despite his kidney trouble, of emerging as the leader of Indian Muslims. Hence the importance of that photograph in Cordova Cathedral, saying *namaz*. Emma Wegenast was still a humble and middle-aged teacher. The gulf, in a social sense, between them had grown so markedly in the intervening quarter of a century as to have become almost unbridgeable. The thread of relationship could not so easily be resumed from the days when they shared a *pension* in Heidelberg and walked on the banks of the river Neckar; when she taught him to read Goethe's *Faust*. It was the story of Thomas Hardy's 'Broken Appointment'—but in reverse. It was the man who 'did not come' in this instance and was thus found wanting not only in loving kindness, but constancy. The woman kept her tryst and proved to be more committed in love. It was no use for Iqbal, in a mood of passionate lamentation to write an immortal line (at least, in the original Urdu, once read never to be forgotten):

> I am the story of the grief of desire,
> And you—the history of the mourning of love.

In real life, however, it turned out to be exactly the obverse.


But then Iqbal always tended to be ambivalent in his relationship with women—and men, and in other matters, too, as we have seen. In his letter to Attia he had written that he wanted to visit Bombay, evidently to seek consolation in her company. But he never went to Bombay that year, although one could travel from Lahore to Bombay and back for less than a hundred rupees in great comfort in those pre-First World War days before the advent of confetti money. Instead of going to Bombay, in February 1910 he took a second wife—Sardar Begum. She seems to have been a charming girl, Kashmiri like Iqbal, and reasonably well-educated according to the standards of the day, especially among the Muslim community. The marriage was duly solemnized.

Wayward if not capricious as ever, after the *nikah* was

performed, Iqbal refused to bring the bride home with him, according to Dr Rafiq Zakaria's book on Iqbal 'due to a misunderstanding'. The 'misunderstanding' was that Iqbal had received a poison-pen letter—or letters—casting aspersions on her character. The letter was anonymous. Iqbal ought to have treated it with the contempt it deserved. Instead, he took the charges against Sardar Begum seriously and punished her by refusing to accept her as his wife. Most of his friends thought his behaviour extraordinarily foolish and unreasonable, but it was not until 1913 that he had another *nikah* ceremony performed, and then only because Sardar Begum threatened him with the wrath of God on Judgement Day. As a true believer, he was particularly mindful of the Day of Judgement, although he had intellectually wrestled with God in his longish poem, *Shikwah* (Complaint) for being so hard and unjust to Muslims.

Meanwhile, he had taken a third wife some time in 1913, the year he remarried Sardar Begum. She was called Mukhtar Begum and was the daughter of a wealthy businessman of Ludhiana. Views about her differ. Some of Iqbal's biographers describe her as a colourless person. On the other hand, he himself told one of his close friends that he liked her the best and that life with her was very heaven, or words to that effect. Anyhow, she did not live long and there was no issue from the marriage. She died in 1924. Iqbal's two remaining children—Jawid Iqbal and Munira Banu—were from Sardar Begum, born in 1924 and 1930 respectively. Jawid Iqbal studied law and eventually became the Chief Justice of Pakistan. What happened to Munira we can only guess. From her photographs which have appeared in various biographies of Iqbal, she seems to have been an attractive and intelligent girl, much like her mother Sardar Begum who died in 1935 when Munira was a child of five and Jawid a boy of eleven.

Iqbal, already ailing from persistent kidney trouble and other incurable afflictions, knew perhaps that he had not long to live. He was naturally worried over the education of his two children by Sardar Begum, especially Jawid of whom he was very fond. This is evident in the letter marked 'confidential', that he wrote on 11 December 1935 to his friend Ross Masood. It was Masood to whom, it is well to recall, E.M. Forster had dedicated his novel *A Passage to India*, and who had for some years been the Vice-Chancellor of Aligarh University, before going on to serve Hamidullah Khan, the Nawab of Bhopal, who unlike the Nizam of Hyderabad, was a man of liberal views and outlook. Masood had also gone with Iqbal on a three-member deputation to Afghanistan at the invitation of the Afghan Government to advise them about educational reforms. The third member of the team was Maulana Suleiman Nadvi.

In his letter to Masood, Iqbal had expressed his anxieties about Jawid and Munira, both minors, if he were to die. As it was probably through the instrumentality of Ross Masood that the Nawab of Bhopal had lately settled a monthly allowance of Rs 500 on Iqbal, he reminded Masood of a conversation he had when in Bhopal, that the monthly allowance of Rs 500 was sufficient for his needs which were few. But at the same time he wondered whether Masood was on corresponding terms with 'His Highness The Aga Khan'. If so, would Masood suggest that the Aga Khan grant a 'pension' to Jawid till he had completed his education or until 'His Highness' deemed fit? He was uncertain, for various reasons, whether a direct appeal to the Aga Khan would elicit a favourable response.

The reasons were transparent enough. He regarded the Aga Khan's leadership of the Muslim delegation at the Round Table Conference at St James' Palace to be flawed—as Jinnah's leadership of the Muslim League was flawed—but in a different way. Besides, towards the last days of his life Iqbal, intellectually and philosophically, was in a somewhat 'purist' not to say 'fundamentalist' frame of mind. He could hardly approve the somewhat latitudinarian attitude to Islam which, as Jawaharlal Nehru said in an article in the *Modern Review* enabled the Aga Khan to reconcile Mecca with Newmarket. This was reproduced in the first bulletin of the Progressive Writers' Association, London in 1936, of course, with Nehru's permission which was readily given to Mulk Raj Anand and myself when we met in his flat in the Artillery Mansion just off Great Victoria Street.

The upshot of any correspondence which Ross Masood had with the Aga Khan was probably negative. But to reassure Iqbal, Masood in a very affectionate letter to him in the middle of June 1937, offered himself, if he were alive, to defray the expenses of Munira's and Jawid's education should the 'Guardians' face any financial problem. He was even prepared to set this down in his will and testament. Evidently, Iqbal had appointed four guardians to look after Munira and Jawid's interests were he to die while they were still minors. Belatedly, he thought of appointing Ross Masood as one of the guardians. That would have meant one of the guardians standing down and there were certain legal complications which he was unable to sort out in time, for within ten months of receiving Masood's letter, Iqbal was no more.

The only wife who survived Iqbal was his first, Karim Bibi. Both husband and wife were of the same age when they married, though gossip had it that she was older, which Aftab denied in the Arshizada interview he gave a few months before his death in 1979. Karim Bibi died in November 1946, a few months before the birth of Pakistan, although the period of gestation was nearly over. As for Aftab, Iqbal had long severed all connections with him. Why Iqbal was so bitterly alienated from his elder son remains something of a mystery. In one of his letter to Kishan Prasad Shad written early in March 1917 he provided a clue. 'The boy,' he wrote, 'is studying in Delhi College. He is brainy and intelligent, but is too fond of fun and games. I'm wondering whether I should place him under a (spiritual) teacher as a "disciple" or get him married' (apparently, to wean him away from his fondness for fun and games). But that does not explain the alienation which progressively grew with the years.

Actually Aftab's academic record was not at all bad. It certainly compared favourably with Iqbal's. Like his father before, Aftab matriculated from Punjab University in the first division in 1916. He joined St Stephen's College in Delhi, it seems without his father's permission, from where he passed his Intermediate examination in the second division in 1918. Thus far the father and the son had parallel records. Aftab, however fared better in BA, graduating in philosophy and sociology with a first division while Iqbal could only manage a second division from Government College, Lahore. After graduation, Aftab decided to go to London, again without consulting his father, and presumably with the funds provided by Karim Bibi's father who was a man of some substance. He did his MA from the London University, joined Lincoln's Inn and was called to the Bar in 1929. Lest that might seem unconscionably long, it should be explained that part of the time he was in the Punjab—from November 1924 to June 1926.

After being called to the Bar, for two years he lived off his wits, earning a meagre pittance by teaching Urdu, then not very much in demand. It was a time of economic crisis in the United Kingdom. Besides, there was not even a pretence of racial equality and it was extremely difficult for a young Indian to establish a legal practice. Aftab got heavily into debt and his 'impecunious condition' was much talked about, especially among the Muslim community which was microscopic when compared to what it has become at the end of the twentieth century. Akbar Hydari, 'Prime Minister' of the Nizam of Hyderabad at the time, happened to be in London as the head of the Hyderabad delegation at the First Round Table Conference at the beginning of January 1931. He heard of the condition in which Aftab was living and wrote at once to Fakhar Yar Jung:

> I have seen Aftab Iqbal and he impressed me very favourably. He [spoke] exceedingly well at a gathering at which Col. Patterson the political ADC to the Secretary of State and several others were present. I should like you very much to kindly help him in the University with regard to examinership and translations. I have written in similar terms to Fazl Mohammad Khan and hope you two together will be able to help this young man who I think will be an asset to the community later on.

On returning to Hyderabad he wrote to Iqbal himself in March 1931, supplicating on Aftab Iqbal's behalf:

> I venture to write to you upon a very delicate subject. Your son Aftab Iqbal appealed to me for help in London and I confess that I was very favourably impressed by him. His impecunious condition was the talk of the Muslim community there. If I was distressed on his account, I was still more distressed on account of the slur or blame which people cast on one whom I have always regarded as a great man and a great Muslim. I do not know the cause of your displeasure with your son, but I do implore you to consider whether it would not be possible for you to give him countenance and help till he is able to maintain himself.

I ask to believe that in making this representation I am animated only by the friendliest motives.

Iqbal did not respond to Akbar Hydari's letter till 2 May. He had the opportunity of meeting Akbar Hydari in Delhi but deliberately avoided doing so, believing that Aftab 'might become the subject of our conversation'. 'The story is long and too painful to relate,' he said, and went on to add:

> I am sure if you had known all the facts you would have found it difficult to write to me on his [Aftab's] behalf... I have already helped him beyond my capacity in spite of the manner in which he has been behaving towards me and other members of our family. No father can read with patience the nasty letter which he has written to us.

It was all, Iqbal wrote, a part of Aftab's 'blackmailing scheme of which he has been availing himself for some time', adding that it was not possible for him to help Aftab:

> I am an old man with indifferent health [which was true enough] with no hope from any side and two small children to provide for. If I had been a rich man I might have done something even though he does not deserve anything.
>
> I suppose you know nothing of my circumstances. Nature has given me certain things and withheld others. I am perfectly contented and my lips have never known a word of complaint. Perhaps you are the first to whom I have written which I have written not before. I hate parading my woes, for the world is on the whole unsympathetic and anybody has not got Sir Akbar's nature possessing a wide range of sympathy. I know you helped him [Aftab] partly because he favourably impressed you and partly because of me. Your generous nature could not have done otherwise...

It is by no means true that Iqbal's lips had never known 'a word of complaint'. Stoicism never came easily to him. Not only did he lodge a complaint against God about the injustices he had done to Muslim nations collectively, but often bemoaned his own fate most piteously, at least in verse which has rarely been equalled and never surpassed. Almost immediately after praising 'Sir Akbar's generous nature' he insinuated a delicate complaint against him. 'But I am sure,' he wrote, 'you would have [done] a far perfect act of kindness, both to myself and to him, if you could have given him a suitable job in Osmania University.' But that was precisely what Akbar Hydari had done. Of course, it was not for him to give 'a suitable job'. That was the prerogative of the University authorities. But as soon as he learnt of Aftab's condition, he had requested Fakhar Yar Jung and Fazl Mohammad Khan to find for Aftab an examinership or work as a translator. Besides, the Hyderabad delegation had met at Hydari's behest and resolved to advance £190 sterling, a very considerable sum in those days, to Aftab.

Akbar Hydari almost immediately replied to Iqbal's letter of 2 May 1931. He apologized for 'quite unwittingly' causing Iqbal pain. 'Believe me,' he wrote, 'had I been conversant with the unpleasant circumstances to which you refer, I should have undoubtedly ignored the appeal. I am most grateful for your warning advice, and venture to express my sympathetic hope that further attempts to so exploit your great and honoured name will be effectively arrested.' Iqbal writing in reply on 14 May gave some specific instances of assistance to Aftab who had been a spendthrift and had been borrowing recklessly:

> This young man has already spent about Rs 70,000 on himself. Out of this sum he borrowed according to his own statement Rs 50,000 from England. I gave Rs 10,000 to his mother and she spent all this on him besides the amount which she and her father gave the boy.
> 
> Only a month or two before his arrival [in India] I was persuaded to give him Rs 1000 and a few days after his arrival in India I received the first letter of one of his creditors in England. With all this he is writing blackmailing letters every now and then. I wanted to spend you a copy of his last letter to me. But I did not do so mainly because I thought you would cease to sympathize with him...

This is hard to believe. Already in his letters to Hydari, Iqbal had done his best to create a strong prejudice against Aftab. His last letter to Akbar Hydari regarding Aftab was written on 2 February 1937, fourteen months before his death. It seems that Aftab had written another letter to Akbari Hydari early in January 1937 in which he dwelt on the 'comparative poverty' in which Iqbal was living and said that his health was poor and that he had not long to live. He had also said that he was 'unable to help me (Aftab)'. 'After all he has done something for the advancement of the Muslim community in India,' he wrote, and continued:

> In fact everybody here thinks that Hyderabad State should be generous enough to keep the poet alive by making a monthly allowance of a reasonable sum of money in his old age.
>
> Nawab Sahib, would you like a future biographer of my father to say that poet Iqbal and his children lived in poverty when Hydari was at the height of his power and influence in Hyderabad State?...

This was too transparent a device to elicit sympathy for Iqbal and, incidentally, for Aftab, to deceive anybody. Hydari did not personally reply to Aftab as he would have done before being warned by Iqbal. He instructed his personal assistant to formally acknowledge his letter, informing him that Sir Akbar 'is most anxious that Sir Mohd. Iqbal's signal services to the nation should be recognized by a suitable allowance in his present state of health', and that he would take 'the earliest possible opportunity for having the matter placed before His Exalted Highness's Government for consideration'.

Meanwhile Iqbal had received a copy of the formal reply which Hydari's personal assistant had sent to Aftab's letter. He did not know who had sent it, but probably it was Aftab himself. Iqbal wrote to Akbar Hydari the following morning. He guessed that Aftab had written to Hydari without his permission and without even informing him. 'I suppose you know that the writer of this letter is a perfect stranger to me and has been so for many years,' he said, and added:

> It is impossible for me to describe how he has behaved in all these years. However, the sole object of the letter I am writing to you is to put you on your guard against this young man who has been a constant source of pain

to me. I cannot conceive of him writing to you or to other friends of mine without having some sort of mischief in his mind. Taking advantage of your good nature he is trying to give you the impression of some sort of reconciliation [between] me and him. Such a thing is impossible and his only object in writing to you is, I believe, to get some money out of you.

He reminded Hydari that Aftab had on an earlier occasion, 'exploited your generous nature' and hoped that Hydari would not encourage him 'to write letters to you any more'. But one more attempt to enlist Akbar Hydari's sympathy for Aftab was made. It was soon after Iqbal's death. Early in May 1938, Sir Mohammad Zafarullah Khan—who was later to become the Foreign Minister of Pakistan—wrote to Hydari from Simla about Aftab Iqbal. He described him as a young man of 'great talent and promise' who was in distress. Zafarullah wanted Hydari to help Aftab because he regarded him as 'a very deserving case'. What response Zafarullah had to his appeal to Hydari we do not know. It is very likely Hydari told him that Iqbal had warned him against Aftab and to turn a deaf ear to any plea for help for him. But it was rather extraordinary that Aftab had sought Zafarullah's help. This up and coming man among the Muslim community who was within less than a decade to become the Foreign Minister of Pakistan was a Qadiani or Ahmediya, a 'heretical' sect of Islam which did not believe in the doctrine of 'finality' of Prophethood, and of which Iqbal did not approve in his later years. But Aftab must have been desperate for money and probably thought that an appeal by Zafarullah to Hydari would be more effective than his own.

The rest is silence, though not quite. *Sha'ir*, the magazine to which reference has been already made, published in its Iqbal special issue (vol. I) two letters written by Aftab after he went to London. They are both addressed to Dr Atta Muhammad, Karim Bibi's father. The first was written from 21 Cromwell Road, South Kensington, and is dated 4 July 1922. It is in Urdu, though it has a postscript as long as the letter, if not longer, in English. It is a straightforward appeal for funds Aftab needed to meet the entrance fee to the University and to buy books, requesting his maternal grandfather to send the money to a certain Miss Buck. He was prepared to execute a bond for it which Dr Atta Muhammad had demanded. The postscript in English is mostly a complaint. He said that it was the 'strongest' letter he had ever received from his maternal grandfather. That he would not have minded. 'You have every right to remonstrate with me in your letters,' he wrote, 'Other people on the contrary ought to be given the impression that I am doing well even if you thought that my mode of living in England was objectionable.' That was why he was surprised that the letter in which Aftab's maternal grandfather had asked for a legal document was in some stranger's handwriting. 'These are strictly private domestic matters,' he wrote, 'and I don't think anybody who does not directly belong to the family ought to know them. I shall be obliged if you write all your letters yourself...I don't want anybody to know my business...' This was an entirely legitimate plea.

The other letter, which is in Urdu and undated, is at once more plaintive and combative. Aftab again repeated that he was asking for a loan, not a gift or prize; he was prepared to execute a bond to repay the sum. The second letter also furnished a clue to his father's anger with him. 'My chief crime in the eyes of my father is,' Aftab claimed, 'that I have always taken the side of my mother. My father knew perfectly well that this is what will happen one day. How could he expect something good out of me when he knew that he was not dealing justly with my mother. He did not expect that you, too, would regard me as criminal.' 'Why,' Aftab asks Dr Atta Muhammad, 'are you so angry with me?' That was true enough. Aftab had always taken his mother's side. Indeed, he had been very unhappy about his father's marrying two wives in quick succession. Although he was a young boy of thirteen or fourteen at the time, he felt deeply hurt for his mother's sake at being 'deserted' by Iqbal. Most of his later pranks and deceits were intended to 'punish' his father.

About a year before his death, Aftab gave a written interview to Akbar Ali Khan Arshizada from Rampur in which he recalled these events. The interview is published in full in the journal *Sha'ir*. With the benefit of hindsight, he changed his position somewhat and even tried to justify Iqbal's conduct. He told Arshizada that Iqbal had called Karim Bibi to him and told her that he had always respected her; that she would be the real mistress of the household; and that Sardar Begum and Mukhtar Begum would do nothing without consulting her wishes. It scarcely sounds convincing and in the Arshizada interview Aftab's testimony tended to be economical with the truth. It is even possible that Iqbal might have said this to Karim Bibi to assuage her feeling of hurt which was long-standing, he having compounded it not only with his infidelities but his indifference, if not worse, towards her. Iqbal had come increasingly to resent his early marriage to her as we know from the letter he wrote to Attia Faizi soon after his return from Europe. He had told Attia that he had thought of fleeing the country, presumably to Germany where he had formed a strong attachment to Emma Wegenast—and she to him. That would have been, indeed, the marriage of true minds.

Perhaps, the indifference to Karim Bibi had set in once the novelty of being married wore off. But the infidelities began soon after he moved to Government College, Lahore. He was young and handsome. Besides, he had the superb gift of poetry, much admired in Lahore society at the turn of the century, especially in Muslim society who always talked poetry and had not yet learned to talk in prose—unlike M. Jourdain in Moliére's *Bourgeois Gentilhonme*. In the early part of this book I referred to his escapades and visits to a certain quarter in Lahore where dance and song were the order of the day or, at any rate, the night.

It was probably during these wanderings that he met Amir, a young and beautiful dancing girl. He fell passionately in love and could not bear to be even momentarily parted from her as is evident in a letter he wrote to Mir Taqi, a boyhood friend and the eldest son of Syed Mir Hassan, Iqbal's teacher who was much more than a teacher—preceptor could be the appropriate term. The letter was written in May 1903 from Mughal Kot, fifty miles from Fort Sandeman, then in the North-West Frontier Province where Iqbal had gone in connection with a case. Towards the end of a brief letter, Iqbal comes to the crux of the matter. He asks Taqi, 'Where is Amir? For God's sake do go there because I'm very troubled.' Then he wrote something that is very reminiscent of a couplet of Momen, one of the galaxy of poets at the court of Bahadur Shah Zafar, the last of the Mughal 'Emperors', a considerable poet, who was a pensioner and later prisoner of the British. The lines of Momen read as follows:

It is as if you are with me
When there's no one else with me.

Iqbal virtually paraphrased it for Taqi, although he was unable to reproduce the lilt and music of Momen's simple, but poignant, words: 'God knows what is the secret,' he wrote, 'the more distant I am from her, the nearer I feel to her'.

Iqbal's friends who knew Amir in her days of power and glory all vouchsafe that she was not only beautiful, but was well-versed in Urdu and Persian poetry as most dancing and singing girls were before the advent of the streetwalkers and call-girls. However, the object of one's heart's desire has nothing to do with her or his merits. Amir may or may not have had all the virtues attributed to her, but Iqbal, unlike Yeats, did not love 'the pilgrim soul' in her, but just what she was—for herself. He felt ill when he did not see her even for a day. On this the testimony of his friends is unanimous and utterly convincing.

Shorash Kashmiri recounts an incident in the journal *Sha'ir's* Iqbal number which was narrated to him by Abdul Majid Salik, who was later to be disenchanted with Iqbal for accepting a knighthood from the British Government. He told him that one day Maulana Ghulam Qadir Girami came to Lahore. Salik was sitting in his office. He wanted to see Iqbal and took Salik with him to Iqbal's house, then in Bazaar Hakiman (Physicians' Street as the locality was known at the time by professionals who worked in that area). Iqbal's old faithful servant, Ali Bakhash, told them that he was ill and lying down. They went in and could see that Iqbal was unkempt and had not shaved for days. His eyes were red with crying. It appeared that he had not seen Amir for several days because her 'mother' had forbidden her visits to Iqbal. On hearing this Girami burst out laughing and said something to Iqbal in Punjabi, the peculiar flavour of which cannot be reproduced in plain English. The gist of what Girami said was, 'You are a hell of a fellow. You want her "mother" to hand over her "cooking pot" to you' (meaning means of livelihood).

However, the Maulana, seeing that Iqbal was in a pitiable condition and in no fit state to appreciate his jokes, asked Ali Bakhash to ready the carriage and took Salik with him to the street where Amir lived (probably Tibbi Bazaar and its environs). They knocked at the door, and it was Amir's 'mother' who opened the door. On seeing Maulana Girami she was pleased and welcomed him. Girami complained that she was bent on killing 'our poet'. She responded:

> What have poets got? A few rhymes and metres and rules of prosody. Do you want me to die of starvation by giving my 'daughter' to your poet? He comes here and stands vigil. If I allow my 'daughter' to go away with him, who is going to take care of me? Tell me...

She, however, eventually relented, seeing Maulana Girami's grey beard, but not until he promised that he would bring Amir back in a couple of hours. She allowed Amir to go to Iqbal's house with Girami and Salik thinking, perhaps, that there was safety in numbers. When they reached there, Girami called out to Iqbal, 'Get up. Amir is here.' When the poet saw Amir standing before him, he could scarcely believe his eyes, but when he realized that he was not dreaming his face lit up.

At the beginning of this biographical chapter, it was suggested that Amir was to Iqbal in his youth what Beata Beatrice was to Dante throughout his life—or nearly. But the parallel seems, on second thoughts, a little far-fetched and ends up in a striking contrast. Not necessarily because of the distance in time that separates the two women, although seven centuries which have passed since Beatrice Portinari—that was her family name—lived have tended to magnify the legendary element surrounding the account of Dante's love for her. Nor is it even in the social class to which each belonged. While Beatrice came from a well-to-do aristocratic family, Amir was a mere dancing girl, a *demi-mondaine* who probably earned her living by the horizontal trade. Still less is it in their life-spans. Beatrice died young in her mid-twenties, while Amir lived on to a ripe old age as Shorash Kashmiri, who saw her when she was aged and infirm—with deep hollows round her eyes, not just creeping shadows which a kind friend comfortingly told Yeats he had seen about the eyes of Yeats' well-beloved—tells us in his brief article in the journal *Sha'ir*.

However, in the final analysis, the difference is in the contrasting attitudes of Dante and Iqbal to the women they loved. Again, it is not that Dante's love for Beatrice was a rare example of Platonic love demanding renunciation while Iqbal's love for Amir was profane, craving for possession. As I have said earlier, both in their intensity admit of no differentiation. Dante, so the legend goes, saw Beatrice when she was nine, crossing the Ponte Vecchio over the Arno at Florence, while Iqbal frequently had the pleasure of Amir's company in the years that he knew her. It is always easier to idealize such chance encounters, especially when there is an aura of early death to cast a glow over one's memory than when one has to live with a creature of flesh and blood over a longer period. Dante has done that and most of his poems in *Vita Nuova* have Beatrice as a source of their anguished inspiration. In *Divina Comedia* itself he takes Beata Beatrice as his ultimate guide to *Paradiso* when Virgil voluntarily admitted that he could guide Dante no further.

On the other hand, Iqbal was too timorous a man to acknowledge in his work his love—or lust which, too, is a kind of loving—for Amir and expunged all traces of her from his verse, although she casts her exquisite shadow over most of his lyrical poetry, both Urdu and Persian. Indeed, her name appears directly only in one of his early poems—'Sarguzshat-e-Adam', or 'Adam's Story'—which was published in 1904 in the journal *Makhzan*, edited by Abdul Qadir, then his most loyal friend, whom Iqbal forgave for certain indiscreet remarks he is supposed to have made to the British high-ups in the Government of India. Iqbal eventually deleted a few lines from the poem and it was included in *Bang-i-Dara*. Indirect references to her, of course, abound; as late as *Jawid Nama*, she figures as Ambapalika, the dancer and courtisan who sold 'pleasure' and whom, Iqbal thought mistakenly, Buddha 'brought to repentance'.

That he should do so, underlines, in a sort of way, the difference between two cultures. Incidentally, it also betrays in Iqbal a tendency to hanker after social respectability, natural enough in the milieu in which he lived and moved and had his being—respectability that has ruined many more lives than Eliza Dolittle's uncle's. Khushwant Singh says somewhere *àpropos* of Iqbal that he was a saint trying hard to be a sinner, or words to that effect. But, perhaps, it was just the reverse: Iqbal might have been an inveterate sinner trying hard to be a saint. Despite his bold claims in his work, he did not have the courage of his sins, except in a very roundabout way, while all true saints, from St Augustine to Gandhi, have had the courage to acknowledge their sins. They would be less of saints without that courage.

Judgement on Iqbal as a man vary. Even his elder son was highly critical of him. He has most of the failings to which flesh is heir, if anything more so and accentuated by the passion with which he pursued them. But the poet in him transcended these taints of ill. Poetry is a gift of the gods and those upon whom they bestow this gift they tend to absolve of all their sins. Who are we mere mortals to sit in judgement on them upon whom the Muses have smiled so bountifully?

# A Short Bibliography

## I. WORKS BY IQBAL

Poetry

> *Asrar-i-Khudi* (Secrets of Self), Persian, 1915
> *Ramuz-i-Bekhudi* (Mysteries of Selflessness), Persian, 1917
> *Payam-i-Mashrik* (Message of the East), Persian, 1923
> *Bang-i-Dara* (The Caravan Bell), Urdu collection, 1924
> *Zabur-i-Ajam* (Psalms of the East), Persian, 1927
> *Jawid Nama* (The Book of Eternity), Persian, 1932
> *Bal-i-Jibreel* (The Wing of Gabriel), Urdu, 1935
> *Zarb-i-Kalim* (The Stroke of Moses), Urdu, 1936
> *Pas Cheh Bayad Kard Ai Aqwam-i-Sharq: Musafir* (What, then, is to be done, O Nations of the East? and The Traveller), Persian, 1937
> *Armughan-i-Hejaz* (The Gift of Hejaz), Urdu and Persian, 1938

Prose

> *The Development of Metaphysics in Persia*, 1908
> *The Reconstruction of Religious Thought in Islam*, 1934
> *Speeches and Statements*, 1944
> *Letters to Jinnah*, 1943

English translations of Iqbal's verse

> *The Secrets of Self*, translated from the Persian by R. A. Nicholson (Macmillan, 1920)
> *The Poppy of Sinai*, translated from the Persian by A. J. Arberry (Royal India Society, 1947)
> *Poems of Iqbal*, translated from the Urdu by Victor Kiernen (Kutub, 1948)

## II. BOOKS ON IQBAL (Selected list)

> Beg, A. Anwar. *The Poet of the East* (Lahore, 1939)
> Enwer, Ishrat Hassan. *The Metaphysics of Iqbal* (Lahore, 1938)
> Saiyidain, K. G. *Iqbal's Educational Philosophy* (Lahore, 1938)
> Sinha Sachchidananda. *Iqbal: The Poet and his Message* (Allahabad, 1947)
> Smith, W. Cantwell. *Modern Islam in India* (Lahore, 1943)
> Vahid, S. A. *Iqbal, His Art and Thoughts* (Lahore, 1944). Second and revised edition (New Delhi, 1989)
> Various authors. *Aspects of Iqbal* (Lahore, 1938)
> Various authors. *Iqbal as a Thinker* (Lahore, 1945)

# Additional Bibliography

Ahmad, D. *Iqbal as I knew him* (Lahore: Iqbal Academy, 1985)
Abdul-Hakim, K. *Fikr-e-Iqbal* (Lahore: Bazm-e-Iqbal, 1964)
Batalvi, A. H. *Iqbal ke Akhari Do Sal* (Lahore: Feroz Sons, 1961)
Begum, A. *Letters of Iqbal to Attia Begum* (English and Urdu texts) (Lahore: Ayynah-i-Adali, 1975)
Chopra, H. L. *Da Ikbal aur unkie Sayari* (Benaras: Hindi Parcharaka Pustaklaya, 1956)
Dar, B. A. *Iqbal and Post-Kantian Voluntarism* (Lahore: Bazm-e-Iqbal, 1956)
Dar, B. A. (ed) *Letters and Writings of Iqbal* (Karachi: Iqbal Academy, 1967)
Iqbal, Jawid. *Zinda-e-Rud* (Lahore: Sheikh G. Ali, 1985)
Jafri, S. H. M. (ed) *Iqbal Fikr-e-Islam Ki Tashkil* (Karachi: Pakistan Study Centre, 1986)
Khan, Y. H. *Ghalib aur Iqbal Ki Mutabarik Jamalyat* (New Delhi: Ghalib Academy, 1979)
Latif, S. M. (ed) *Speeches, Writings and Statements of Iqbal* (Lahore, 1974)
Saeed, S. M. (ed) *Reconstruction of Religious Thought in Islam* (Lahore: Institute of Islamic Culture, 1986)
Schimmel, A. *Gabriel's Wing* (Bill Leiden, 1963)
Sharif, M. M. *About Iqbal and his Thought* (Lahore: Institute of Islamic Culture, 1964)
Zakaria, Rafiq *Iqbal* (New Delhi: Viking Books, 1993)

Urdu Magazines: Some Special Numbers on Iqbal

*Ajkal*, November 1977, Publications Division, New Delhi
*Huma*, October 1976, Jungpura Extension, New Delhi
*Mah-e-Nau*, April 1970, Matbuat-e-Pakistan, Karachi
*Narang-e-Khyal*, January 1932, 1942, Narang-e-Khyal, Lahore
*Nuqush*, September 1977, December 1977, Idara Farag-e-Urdu, Lahore
*Sha'ir*, January–June 1988, Qasr-ul-Adab, Bombay

(Prepared by Dr Fakhir Hussain)

# Index

Abdul Qadir, Sheikh 17-18, 21-2, 25, 150-1, 171
Abdul Quddas Gangoh 106
Abu Jahal 115
Afghanistan 38, 66-7, 125, 160
Afghan War, Third 67
Africa 31, 39, 60
Aftab, Iqbal 148, 150-5, 161-8
  *See* Iqbal, Mohammed; Karim Bibi; Muhammad Atta
Aga Khan 160
Agnosticism 23
Ahmed Khan, Sir Saiyed 12, 14, 20-1, 57, 155
Ahmediya 166, *see* Qadiani
Ahriman 115
Ajmal Khan, Hakim 149
Akbar Hydari 79-80, 162-6
Akbar of Allahabad 28
*Al Hilal* 37
Ali Bakhash 18, 133, 152, 169
Ali brothers 37, 149
Aligarh 13, 141
Aligarh College and University 12, 155, 159
Aligarh Movement 12-14, 36, 57, 108
*A Literary History of Persia* 24
All-India Muslim Conference 92
All-India Muslim League *See* Muslim League
Altaf Husain Hali of Panipat *See* Hali
Ambala Division 90
Ambapalika 171
Amir 148, 168-71
Amir Aman Ullah Khan 66-7
Amritsar 149

*Ana'l Haqq* (I am the Truth) 116
Anand, Mulk Raj 160
Anarkali, Lahore 9, 124
Andalusia 31
Anglo-Sikh War, Second 1
Anjuman-i-Himayat-i-Islam (Society for the aid of Islam) 13, 40-1, 46-7, 74, 81, 128
Ansari, Dr 37
*A Passage to India* 159
Arabia 31, 51, 61, 68, 90, 137
Aristotle 49
*Armughan-i-Hejaz* (The Gift of Hejaz) 122
Arnold, Sir Thomas 15-17, 19, 22, 27, 65
Arshizada, Akbar Ali Khan 151, 153, 167-8
Arya Samaj 151
*Asiri* (Slavery) 149
*Aspects of Iqbal* 137
*Asrar-i-Khudi* (Secrets of Self) 47-8, 50-2, 56-7, 59, 63-5, 68-9, 75, 100, 102, 106, 123
Ataturk, Kemal 62, 67, 70, 113
Attia Faizi, Begum 28, 148-9, 155-6, 158, 168
Azim Hussain 75, 78-80, 82
  *See* Fazl-i-Hussain

Baal 115
Bahadur Shah Zafar 168
Baldwin, Stanley 153
*Bal-i-Jibreel* (The Wing of Gabriel) 110, 122-3, 141
Baluchistan 89
*Bang-i-Dara* (The Caravan Bell) 10, 171

Beatrice, Beata (née Portinari) 112, 148, 170–1
Beaverbrook, William 153
Bengal 36–7, 91, 119, 136
Bergson 24, 54, 70
Bhartrihari 119, 122
Bhopal 131, 160, see Nawab of Bhopal
Bombay 127, 156, 158
Bosanquet, Bernard 24
Boswell, James 21, 127
*Bourgeois Gentilhomme* 168
Bradley, Francis Herbert 24
Brahmo Samaj 12
British
    Conquest 119
    Empire 29, 89–90, 141, 150
    Government 65, 79–80, 140, 169
    Imperialism 150
British Proconsul 80, 125
Browne, E.G. 24, 63
Browning, Robert 70
Brunetto, Master 113
Buck, Miss 166
Buddha, Gautama 115, 171
Bulleh Shah 133
Byron, Lord George Gordon 70

Caliphate 31, 38, 60–1, 65, 113, 115. See also Khilafat
Cambridge 23–4, 27, 32
Capitalism 63, 115, 142, 152
*Categories* 49
Charles V 110
Chaudhri Shahab-ud-Din 78
Chaudhri Zafrullah Khan 78
Christendom 60, 96, 113
Christianity 86–8, 107, 111, 113
Church Militant 109, 157
Churchill, Winston 153–4
Civil Lines, Lahore 9
'Complaint' 39
Communalism 65, 89

Communism 90
Congress 61, 149, 151. See also Indian National Congress
Congress leaders 80, 94. See also Hindu leadership
Conservative Party 153. See also Tory Party
Constantine 107
Constitutional Reforms in India 153
Cordova 109, 157–8. See also Mosque of Cordova
'Cry of the Orphan' 40
Curzon, Lord 36

Dacca 36
Dagh 6, 7, 41
Dante 33, 111–13, 148, 170–1
Daoud, Ibrahim Poure 122
*Das Kapital* 115
Dayananda, Swamy 151
*De Civitate Dei* 142
Delhi 3, 10, 63, 73, 127, 129, 161
'Dialogue between Love and Knowledge' 70
'Dialogue between God and Man' 70
*Discovery of India* 93, 152
*Divina Comedia* 111–13, 171
Divine Viceregency 54, 55, 144 See also Naib; Niyabat-i-Ilahi
Diwan Ali 133
Donne, John 148

Eastern mysticism 23
Eastern Movement in German Letters 66
Ego (Khudi or Self) 52–5, 57, 105, 119–21, 142–4. See also Divine Viceregency
Egypt 38, 109, 125
Einstein, Albert 70
Eliot, Thomas Stearns 84
Empire of Rome 44. See also Rome

# Index

England 19, 20, 23–4, 27, 29, 32, 63–4, 78, 125, 157, 164, 167
English
   Literature 15
   Romantics 10, 17
Europe 17, 19, 21, 25, 29, 30–2, 34, 38–9, 43, 60, 67, 87, 96, 98, 105, 109–10, 125, 129, 156, 168
European Romantics 136

Fakhar Yar Jung 162, 164
*Faust* 158
Fazl-i-Hussain 75, 78, 79–82, 150–2
   son of *See* Azim Hussain
Fazl Mohammad Khan 162, 164
Federal Structure Committee 79
Fitzgerald, Edward 64
Florence 171
Forster, E. M. 63, 159
Fort Sandeman 168
Frauleins Wegenast, Senechal and Schat 27–8. *See also* Wegenast, Fraulein Emma
Freud, Sigmund 113

Gabriel 110, 119, 122–3
Gandhi, Mohandas Karamchand 20–1, 134, 139, 171
Garratt, G. T. 37
German philosophy and literature 27, 66. *See also* Kant; Hegel
Germany 21, 23, 27, 29, 156, 168
*Ghazal* 48, 70
Ghazali 106
Ghalib, Mirza 116–17
Ghani 119
Ghazni 125
Girami, Moulana Ghulam Qadir 169–70
Goethe 27, 66, 70, 158
Government of India Act 153
Government College, Lahore 7, 9, 15–17, 34–5, 45, 150, 155, 161, 168
Governor-General of India 150

Greek thought and ideas 49, 50, 106, 131. *See also* Plato

Hafiz 24, 42, 47, 50, 66
Hailey, Malcolm 75
*Hakims* (indigenous medicine men) 132
Hakim Mohammed Hussain 132
Hakim Nabeena 132
Hali 12, 41, 137
Halifax, Lord *See* Irwin
'Hamara Hindustan' (Our India) 15
Hamidullah Khan 159
Hardy, Thomas 158
Hegel, Georg Wilhelm Friedrich 23–4, 27, 54, 70
Heidelberg 27–8, 148, 156–8
Hejaz 125
Hindus 3, 12, 36–7, 50, 61, 65, 89–92, 140, 150–2, 162
   intelligentsia 11
   leadership 61, 92, 94. *See also* Congress Leaders
   middle class 36, 77
   bourgeoisie 91
   Renaissance 109
Hinduism 109, 157
Home Rule 61
Huxley, Aldous 23, 156
Hyderabad 7, 80–1, 83, 162, 164–5

Ibn-i-Khaldun 106
Ibn-i-Maskwaih 106
Ibnu-l-Arabi 111–12
*ijtihad* (to exert) 107
Imam Bibi 155
   *See also* Iqbal, Mohammed
Imperialism 29, 38, 63, 90, 141, 150
India 1–3, 7, 10–12, 14, 16, 20, 27, 32–6, 38–9, 41–2, 64, 67, 74–5, 79–80, 82, 85–8, 90–2, 118–19, 122, 125–6, 132, 134, 139–40, 147, 152–3, 155–7, 165

Indian freedom 61
   independence struggle 36
     *See also* Nationalism
   intelligentsia, role of 20, 63, 65
   middle class, role of 20, 33, 64, 77
   Muslims, role of 37, 66, 76, 80, 86, 90, 96, 152, 158
Indian National Congress 13, 14
   *See also* Congress
Indian nationalism 13, 14, 29, 36
   *See also* Nationalism
   national movement 14, 36
Indo-Anglian Literature 27
Indo-Muslim Renaissance 134, 145
Indo-Persian poetry and literature 27, 67, 139
Iqbal, Mohammed
   association with Anjuman *See* Anjuman-i-Himayat-i-Islam (Society for the aid of Islam)
   birth date 2, 148
   birth place 2, *see* Sialkot
   British government, attitude towards 65, 75–6, 80, 83, 141, 150
   brother 132, 154, *see* Mohammed, Atta
   childhood 5
   Creator of Pakistan 85–92, 94–6, 98, 152–4
   crisis of Islam and Iqbal's poetry 35–8, 65
   daughters 148, *see* Meraj; Munira Begum
   death of 133–4, 161
   education 4, 6, 7, 9–10, 15–17, 20, 23–4, 27–8, 32, 150, 154, 161
   England and European experience 21–5, 27, 32, 34–5, 79, 83, 125, 149, 156–8
   ethical and spiritual ideals 143–6
   evolution of thought *See* philosophy of Iqbal
   father 5, 18, 27, 128, 131, 154–5. *See also* Mohammed, Sheikh Nur
   father-in-law *See* Muhammad, Atta
   family life 130–1, 147–8, 154–6, 159
   failing health and last days 124–5, 130–3, 159, 161
   genealogy 2
   influence of Aligarh Movement and nationalism 13, 29
   inner life of turmoil 46, 97–8, 138, 147. *See also Asrar-i-Khudi*
   Joint editor of *Law Journal* 155
   Knighthood 64–5, 150
   legal profession 35, 45–6, 74, 126
   literary and philosophic controversy 47
   loves 148, 168–71. *See also* Attia Faizi; Amir
   marriages 147–8, 154–5, 15–59, 167–8
   'Message of' 71, 99
   mother 5, 6, 155. *See also* Imam Bibi
   Parallelism of *Divina Comedia* and *Jawid Nama* 111–13
   personality 46, 125–30, 147–50, 172
   Philosopher and Poet of Pakistan 96, 125, 135
   Philosophy of action and creative dynamism 31, 45, 50, 57, 59, 73, 98, 103

*See also* Islamic history,
'the principle of
Movement' in
Philosophy of Egohood 62
*See also* Ego; *Naib*;
*Niyabat-i-Ilahi*
Philosophy of life 51–7. *See*
*Asrar-i-Khudi*
Philosophy of Love 53–4,
71–2, 100–4
poet and prophet 82, 135,
139–43, 146
Poet of Islam 80, 89, 145
politics 29, 61, 76, 78,
81–6, 93–4, 97–8, 151
popularity 41, 126–7, 146
public life 75–86, 91, 98, 128
*See also* Round Table
Conference
returns to India 32–3
Socialism, attitude towards
141. *See also* Socialism
sons *See* Aftab Iqbal; Jawid
Iqbal
spiritual crisis 22, 33, 35–6, 38
starts writing poetry 6–7
teachers of 6, *see* Mir
Hassan, Moulvi; Arnold,
Sir Thomas
Wegenast, Fraulein
Emma
teaching profession 15, 17,
18, 19, 34–5, 45, 155
vision of Islam 127–8. *See also*
*Reconstruction of Religious*
*Thought in Islam*
visit to Afghanistan, Egypt,
Iberian Peninsula and
Palestine 125
wives 150. *See also* Karim
Bibi; Sardar Begum;
Mukhtar Begum
women, attitude towards 5,
27–8, 170–1

Iranian Cultural Mission 122
Irwin (later Lord Halifax) 150
*Ishq* (love) 54
Islam 31, 37–8, 43, 46, 49–50,
59–60, 63, 73, 86–90, 92–3,
95–6, 104–9, 111–13, 121, 127,
129, 132, 140, 144–5, 166. *See*
*also* Pan-Islamism
Islamic Commonwealth 38, 61
culture 6, 87, 104–6
*Islamic Culture* 23
Islamic history 31, 77
Internationalism 68
political crisis in the world
of 35–7, 60–2
'the principle of
Movement' in 107
Italy 109

Jalal-u-Din Rumi *See* Rumi
Jamia Millia, Delhi 129
Jammu and Kashmir 1. *See also*
Kashmir
Jawid Iqbal 111, 120–1, 124, 131,
148, 159–60. *See also* Iqbal,
Mohammed; Sardar Begum
Jawid Manzal 124, 134
*Jawid Nama* (Book of Eternity)
111–13, 115, 117, 120–1, 171
Jesus 87, 115
Jinnah 92, 93–4, 135, 151–4, 160
Jinnah, Fatima 152
Job 39
Julian, Emperor 107

Ka'ba 39, 68, 115
Kaiser Wilhelm II 141
Kangra 18
Kant, Emmanuel 23, 27, 70
Kapilavastu 115
Karim Bibi 147, 154–6, 161, 164,
166–8
Kashmir 2, 119, 125, 129, 158
Kashmiri Brahmins 2

Khilafat 61, 65, 76. *See also* Caliphate
Kierkegaard, Soren 46
King's Mosque, Lahore 41, 128, 134

Lahore 7, 9, 10, 11, 13, 15–6, 29, 34, 45–6, 74, 92–3, 124–5, 128, 130, 134, 148, 150, 152, 155, 156, 158, 168–9
Lahore College of Greek Medicine 132
*Law Journal* 155
Lawrence, D. H. 135
League of Nations 70, 79, 83
Legacy of Islam 48, 112
Leibnitz, Gottfried Wilhelm von 24
Lenin, Vladimir Ilyich 70, 141
Locke, John 70
London 21, 25, 76, 79, 83, 91, 148, 153, 157, 160–2, 166
Lucknow 10, 63
Ludhiana 159
Luther, Martin 87

Macleod Road, Lahore 124
Macmillan, Harold 63
Madrid 157
Magian Complex 107
*Magna Moralia* 49
*Makhzan* 17, 18, 151, 171
Malerkotla 154
Mamun-al-Rashid, Abbasid Caliph or Mamun the Great 49
Marx, Karl 23, 59, 70, 113
Masood, Sir Ross 125, 159, 160–1
*Mathnawi* 48, 59
*Mathnawi-i-Ma'nawi* 48, 52
Mayo, Lord 125
Mayo Road, Lahore 125
McTaggart, Professor 23, 24, 51
Mecca 20, 44, 125, 160
Meraj, Begum 148, 155. *See also* Iqbal, Mohammed, Karim Bibi

Messianic complex 107
Milton, John 25, 111
Minto, Lord 37
Mir Hassan, Moulvi Syed 4–8, 17, 65, 154. *See also* Mir Taqi
Mir Jafar 119, 140
Mir Taqi 168–9
*Miraj* (Ascension of the Prophet) 111, 114
Mirza Arshad of Gurgaon 11
Mission College, Sialkot 7
Mission School, Sialkot 4
*Modern Islam in India* 142
*Modern Review* 160
Moghul Empire 2
Mohammed Ali 36
Mohammed, Atta 4, 154, 156
Molière 168
Momen 168–9
*Monsieur Nicolas* 101
Morley-Minto Reforms 37
Moses 56, 68, 120
Mosque of Cordova 109–10, 129
Moulana Abul Kalam Azad 36–7
Moulana Shibli 37
Mount Sinai 68
Muhammad, Atta 154, 156, 161, 166–7
Muhammad of Arabia 106
Mukhtar Begum 147, 159, 167 *See also* Iqbal, Mohammed
Munich 28
Munira Banu, Begum 131, 148, 159–60. *See also* Iqbal, Mohammed; Sardar Begum
*Murder in the Cathedral* 84
*Musaddas* 12
Muslim community 13, 35, 41, 91, 93, 140, 154, 162, 165–6
Muslim Conference 92, 98
Muslim League 37, 79, 85, 88, 92–3, 95, 98, 149, 151–3, 160. *See also* All-India Muslim League

# Index

Mutiny 4. *See also* Revolt of 1857
Mysore 119, 127

Nadir Shah Abdali 67, 119
*Naib* (Divine Viceregent) 55
National Anthem 15, *see* 'Hamara Hindustan'
Nationalism 14, 29, 30, 37, 63, 65, 86, 140. *See also* Indian nationalism
National Movement 14
Near and Middle East 31, 37-8
Near East 60, 110
Nehru, Jawaharlal 20-1, 90, 93, 152, 160
Nehru, Motilal 149
Neo-Platonism 68, 143
Nestorian 49
*New Era* 60
Nicholson, R. A. 48, 50, 52, 63, 64, 111
Nietzsche Friedrich Wilhelm 24, 46, 54-5, 60, 70, 119, 129
*Nikah* 158-9
*Niyabat-i-Ilahi* (Divine Viceregency) 55
Nizam of Hyderabad 80, 83, 160, 162
Nizam's Government 81, 165
Nizami (Persian Poet) 66
North Sea island 1, 3, 36
North-West Frontier Province 89, 125, 150, 168
North West Muslim State in India 92

O'Dwyer, Michael 149
Omar Khayam 64
Oriental College, Lahore 15, 17
*Ost Westerliche Diwan* 66
Ottoman Empire 37, 39, 60

Pakistan 1, 26, 85, 91-6, 135, 140, 147, 153-4, 159, 161, 166
 Chief Justice of 159. *See also* Jawid Iqbal
 creation of 92, 95; 153-4. *See also* Iqbal, Mohammed
 Philosopher and Poet of 96, 125, 135
Palacios, Asin 111
Palestine 125
Pan-Islamism 38, 65, 93, 115, 135
*Paradise Lost* 25, 111
Patterson, Col. 162
*Payam-i-Mashriq* (Message of the East) 66-9, 71, 73, 75, 83, 141
Persia 25, 37, 51
Persian poetry 6, 10, 21, 26-7, 47-8, 66, 98-9, 122, 135-7, 169, 171
Philosophy 12, 30, 50-1, 59, 75-7, 98, 106, 115, 121
Plato 24, 49-50, 53, 84. *See also Republic*
Ponte Vecchio 171
Prince of Hyderabad 7
Privy Council 153
Progressive Writers' Association 160
Provincial Legislative Council 75-6, 83, 98
Public Services Commission 80
Punjab 1, 8, 18, 73, 75, 78, 82, 89, 93-5, 125, 149, 151-6, 158
 High Court of 75
 land of five rivers 13, 73
 Legislative Council of 78
Purdah 5, 28, 112

Qadiani 93. *See also* Ahmediya
Qu'ran 2, 14, 18, 38, 49, 50-1, 54, 57, 73, 93, 105-7, 111, 115, 121, 127-8, 132, 144

Read, Herbert 63
*Reconstruction of Religious Thought in Islam* 104-5, 108-9

Renaissance 34, 144
*Republic* 49, see Plato
Restif 101, see *Monsieur Nicolas*
Revolt of 1857 (Mutiny) 3, 4, 12
Richards, I. A. 137
Rilke, Rainer Maria 144
*Rise and Fulfilment of British Rule in India* 37
Rolland, Romain 74
Rome 107, see Empire of Rome
Round Table Conference 79, 83, 91, 98, 109–10, 125, 149, 157, 160, 162
Rousseau, Jean Jacques 87, 142
Roy, Raja Rammohan 11–12, 20–1, 109, 139
Rumi, Jalal-u-Din 24, 48, 52, 62, 70, 72, 99, 112–14, 120
Ruskin, John 9

Sadi 66
Saint Simon 142
Saiyad Ahmed Khan 139
Saiyed Ali Hamadani 119
Saiyed Halim Pasha 115
Saiyed Jamal-ud-Din Afghani 38, 115
Salik, Abdul Majid 169, 170
Sapru 2, see Kashmiri Brahmins
Sardar Begum 147, 158–9, 167
'Sarguzshat-e-Adam' (Adam's story) 171
Schiller, Ferdinand Canning Scott 27
Schopenhauer, Johann Christoph Friedrich von 27, 70
Secretary of State for India 78, 79, 162
Seringapatam 119
Sermon on the Mount 43
Shabistvi, Mahmud 99
Shad, Kishan Prasad 161
Shafi, Muhammad 151
*Sha'ir* 151, 166–7, 169–70
*Shams-ul-Ulema* 65

Sharif, M. M. 23
Sher Mohammed, Mian 129–30
Shiraz 18
'Shorash Kashmiri' 169–70
Sialkot 1, 5, 8, 154
Singh, Khushwant 171
Sinha, Sachchidananda 26
Smith, W. Cantwell 142, 145
Socialism 30, 59, 63, 115, 141–2
Soviet Union 67
Spain 109, 157
Spinoza, Benedict de 24
St Augustine 142, 171. See also *De Civitate Dei*
St Stephen's College, Delhi 161
Sufism 50, 52–3
Sufi Persia 25
    poets 42, 50
    poets of Persia 17, 24, 50
    mysticism 68, 143
    mystics 42, 44, 50, 68
Suleiman Nadvi 125, 160
*Summa Theologica* 113

Tabriz 2, 24
Tagore, Rabindranath 6, 20–1, 26, 29, 35, 64–5, 109, 125, 135
*Talu-i-Islam* (The Dawn of Islam) 65–6
Tarik 31, 51, 96, 109
*Tarjumanu-l-Ashwaq* 112
Tartars 68
Taseer, M. D. 137, 141
*The Ardent Pilgrim* 147
'The Book of Bondage' 99. See also *Zabur-i-Ajam*
'The Tulip of Sinai' 67, 69, 72 See also *Payam*
Thompson, Edward 37, 91, 140
*Thus Spake Zarathustra* 54
*Timeus* 49
Tipu Sultan 119
Tolstoy, Leo 115

Tory Party 153. *See also*
    Conservative Party
*Tresor* 113
Tripoli 37, 39, 41

United Kingdom 162
United Provinces 12, 127
Urdu 15, 17, 18, 25–6, 28, 47, 127,
    151, 154, 162, 166–7
    poetry and literature 6, 7,
        10, 17, 21, 25–6, 46, 63,
        65, 98, 110, 122, 135–7,
        169, 171
Utopia 116, 142

Vedanta 50, 53, 68, 127
Vedantic Idealism 143
Vedantists 68
Vedas 2
Venice 157
Venus 11, 115–16
Versailles 21

Victorian Age 23
    prosperity 29
Virgil 33, 112, 171
*Vita Nuova* 171

Ward, James 23
Wegenast, Fraulein Emma 148,
    156–8, 168
Wells, H. G. 84
World War, First 20, 29, 34, 43,
    60–1, 64–5, 150, 156, 158

Yeats W. B. 69, 125, 149, 169–70

*Zabur-i-Ajam* (Psalms of the East)
    99, 100–1, 103–4, 121–2
Zafarullah Khan, Sir Mohammad
    166
Zamora, Alcola 109
*Zarb-i-Kaleem* (The Stroke of the
    Rod of Moses) 122
Zakaria, Rafiq 148–9, 159